D1375971

HOW TO CHOOSE A BIBLE VERSION

An Introductory Guide to English Translations

Robert L. Thomas

Mentor

Christian Focus Publications publishes biblically-accurate books for adults and children. The books in the adult range are published in three imprints.

Christian Heritage contains classic writings from the past.

Christian Focus contains popular works including biographies, commentaries, doctrine, and Christian living.

Mentor focuses on books written at a level suitable for Bible College and seminary students, pastors, and others; the imprint includes commentaries, doctrinal studies, examination of current issues, and church history.

For a free catalogue of all our titles, please write to
Christian Focus Publications,
Geanies House, Fearn,
Ross-shire, IV20 1TW, Great Britain

For details of our titles visit us on our web site
http://www.christianfocus.com

© Robert L. Thomas
ISBN 1 85792 496 7

Published in 2000 by
Christian Focus Publications
Geanies House, Fearn, Ross-shire,
IV20 1TW, Great Britain

Cover design by Owen Daily

Contents

In memory of Dewey Lockman
whose interest in Bible translations
fueled my motivation for this study

INTRODUCTION

The Bible is of greatest importance in the life of every Christian. It is the one and only means of receiving authoritative and specific communication from his/her God. It is the chief weapon in the spiritual conflict that he/she wages from day to day.

English-speaking Christians face a unique challenge, that of choosing which version of the Bible they will use. The multiple options available to them pose a problem of immense proportions, which has never before existed in the history of the Christian church, or at least, has not existed in the same degree of complexity as it does at the beginning of the twenty-first century. The availability of so many translations of the Bible in the English language creates an unparalleled dilemma. The existence of many versions is advantageous in making the gospel known more widely, but it is disadvantageous because a choice of the 'best' translation for regular use becomes more complex.

Teaching everyone the original languages of Scripture is the ideal solution to the problem, but it is not a practical one. Translations of the Bible into various languages have been God's way of getting the gospel message to people throughout the centuries of Christian history. Dependence on those translations puts the average Christian into a position of having to evaluate the possibilities and choose which version he will adopt as his major resource.

A number of excellent books about translations have provided a wealth of details regarding individual translations and are valuable resources. Other works have specialized in one phase or another of Bible translating. Yet little or nothing has presented a full picture of relevant information by placing the versions side-by-side in a manner that allows them to be compared systematically in the relevant spheres of comparison.

Data regarding translations fall into distinct categories, allowing each version to be evaluated category by category. Examining translations in such groupings of information rather than lumping dissimilar kinds of information together provides a clearer picture of the distinctives of each one. That method is far superior to trying to derive sound conclusions from a process that mixes categories.

A knowledge of suitable categories of comparison can greatly aid the average Christian in drawing a better picture of the strengths and weaknesses of various available versions. A degree of expertise is necessary in each area of evaluation. Only years of background study can make one a proficient independent evaluator in any one of the areas. Yet a knowledge of what kinds of information are relevant combined with the opinions of those who have worked in the individual areas can impart considerable confidence to the non-expert in helping him choose a personal translation.

The survey presented in the following pages will introduce broad subject-areas related to English versions. It is only a survey and tries to be suggestive, not exhaustive, in relaying types of information about individual Bible versions. The survey's main function is to categorize the types of information relevant to one's choice of a version for personal use. Though the survey is not sufficient to provide a degree of expertise required to form independent judgments in any one of the areas, it will establish categories for discussion and pinpoint which elements are the main considerations in each category. Such guidelines will allow the task of evaluation to proceed in an orderly and profitable way. Further, if this discussion can whet a reader's appetite to delve into one or more of the areas in detail, another goal of this work will have been met.

FIELDS RELEVANT TO AN
EVALUATION OF BIBLE TRANSLATIONS

Practically everything, if not everything, that has been written or said about Bible translations falls under five headings. Each of the five plays a significant role in determining the value of a version. It is not the purpose of this treatment to lead readers to a final decision as to which version is 'best' in each category of discussion. Deciding what is best must be a personal decision. Though a preference may be implicit in various discussions, the preference will emerge only after what is hopefully a balanced description of the issues involved. This will permit each person to evaluate versions in light of his own personal objectives in the use of an English Bible translation.

1. Historical Backgrounds of Bible Translations
How, when, where, and with whom a translation of the Bible originated is certainly significant. Was it produced by an individual or a committee? Has it been around a long time, or is it of recent vintage? Is its beginning connected with my confessional standards, or did it spring from some other? Those are among the many questions that one may and should ask about the origin of a Bible version when searching to find the best version as a guide for life.

2. Textual Bases of Bible Translations
The ultimate basis for every Bible translation is a language other than English – Hebrew and Aramaic in the Old Testament and Greek in the New Testament. Excellent copies of the original works that came from the hands of the authors are available, but these copies do not always agree with one another in every detail. The Greek New Testament has many more resource manuscripts than the Hebrew and Aramaic Old

Testament, so the disagreements are particularly problematic in establishing the exact wording of the New Testament. Decisions regarding which variations to follow are necessary when making English translations, because in many cases the choices affect English renderings. A person will want a version that bases its English renderings on wise choices from among the variations in the various sources.

3. Methodological Techniques of Bible Translations

This century has witnessed the development of a somewhat new approach to Bible translating. The traditional method renders English translations that correspond as nearly as possible to original-language vocabulary and grammatical constructions. That technique has given way in some quarters to free translations and paraphrases which convey the *translators' understanding of the ideas*. The result is a translation into English words and sentences that sometimes do not approximate the form of the source languages. Both the traditional approach and the newer one have advantages and disadvantages. A reader needs to decide between the two options in light of the way he intends to use Scripture. Well-known translations of both types are available, and one will need to determine at some point which route to follow.

4. Theological Biases of Bible Translations

As hard as a translator may try, it is impossible to exclude theological bias from a translation. At times a choice of renderings will boil down to a doctrinal preference. That is the nature of changing a message from one language to another. Of course, sometimes translators may insert doctrinal preferences intentionally as in the case of study Bibles. A Bible user needs to be aware, at least in a general way, of what theological bias or biases occur in a version before settling upon one as his constant resource. Otherwise, he may unknowingly buy into a teaching that does not agree with his own convictions.

5. Varieties of English in Bible Translations

Ways to communicate a message in English constitute the largest field among the five categories under consideration. Different people respond favorably to different types of English. A single word choice has often been the occasion of many hours of discussion among translators. Choosing from among many possibilities the best way to state a proposition in order to produce maximum understanding among listeners or readers is crucial. Some prefer a paragraph format for the text because it is customary in other types of literature, but others like the verse divisions as individual units with the verse number at the beginning. 'Which is best for me and my purposes?' each person must ask and answer. These are samples of multiplied issues that relate to the matter of English usage.

Since each of the five subjects is a major topic for discussion in itself and one book attempting to deal with all five cannot possibly answer all the important questions, a supplemental reading list appears at the end of each chapter to provide further resources. In these lists are works that supply additional information relevant to matters discussed in that chapter.

The remarks to come should be sufficient to answer many questions and to inform readers in a general way. Then they can deal more specifically with issues that will lead them to choices of versions of the Bible that will best meet their own needs.

Chapter 1

HISTORICAL BACKGROUNDS
OF BIBLE TRANSLATIONS

Broadly speaking, from a historical standpoint, two categories of English translations exist. One category consists of those works that fall within the mainline tradition of the English-speaking church since the sixteenth century, the Tyndale tradition. The other category consists of a wide variety of translations that have no substantial underlying tradition.

THE TYNDALE TRADITION
OF ENGLISH TRANSLATIONS

The work of John Wycliffe deserves initial mention, though Wycliffe's work does not strictly speaking lie within the longstanding tradition of English translations. Wycliffe was the earliest leader to realise that the whole Bible was applicable to all of life and should therefore be available to all men in their own languages. He sponsored a work to translate the Bible into English from the Latin Vulgate, some time in the early 1380s. The translation bears his name, though associates who were part of the movement that he led probably did the translating. Since the printing press did not exist in his time, the work had to be copied by hand. Because of his bold move, government officials confined Wycliffe to his rectory for the last one and a half years of his life.

In the 1390s, John Purvey revised the initial translation and issued a later edition in 1395 or 1396. Purvey's work was a freer translation than the original work had been, since the earlier work was so literal that its English was stilted. Because of his part in the work, officials imprisoned Purvey, and some of his associates died at the stake as heretics. In 1408 a clergy senate prohibited the translation and the reading of any vernacular version of the Bible in whole or in part except by special permission. In spite of the prohibition, the translation grew in popularity.

The organized church opposed a vernacular Bible because of a feeling that Latin was the proper language for religious expression, and English was an inappropriate medium for such. Also, the church leaders feared that false teaching might result if the Bible was in the hands of the laity. In spite of this official action by the church, the Wycliffe translation seems to have gained a degree of popularity by the 1500s.

The Tyndale Version
The earliest translation project of William Tyndale brought into English the Dutch work of Erasmus entitled *The Christian Soldier's Handbook*. The church was at the point of charging Tyndale with heresy for doing so because Erasmus' work promoted the duty of studying the New Testament, and making it the authoritative word in life and doctrine. Nevertheless, Tyndale was firm in his conviction that religious confusion in his day stemmed from a widespread ignorance of the Scriptures, even on the part of many of the clergy. When he undertook a translation of the New Testament, he had to leave England and take up residence in Germany and France to do the work. Even there he found opposition but was finally able to complete the New Testament and have it printed in Worms. It became available in England in 1526. When the work arrived in England, the Bishop of London tried to seize all the copies and burn them in a public place. The destructive campaign was a failure, however. The money the Bishop used to buy up all the copies was used to print more copies of Tyndale's English New Testament.

No direct evidence exists that Tyndale was acquainted with Wycliffe's translation, though some places in his translations have the same expressions as Wycliffe's. Probably a copy of Wycliffe's handwritten Bible had not fallen into his hands because of its limited circulation.

Tyndale continued to work on translation after his New Testament first appeared. The revision of his New Testament that appeared in November of 1534 is the landmark edition. He also translated portions of the Old Testament from Hebrew, including the Pentateuch, Joshua through 2 Chronicles, and Jonah. The Old Testament portions first surfaced as a part of Matthew's Bible in 1537. Tyndale also translated portions of the prophetic and poetic books of the Old Testament, but none in its entirety.

The basis for his translation of the New Testament was the third printed edition of Erasmus' Greek Testament, which appeared in 1522. Tyndale was a good Greek scholar and produced an excellent translation, over ninety percent of which the King James Version retained even after a number of steps of revision between Tyndale and the King James Version. In 1535 Tyndale was kidnapped from the free city of Antwerp and imprisoned. He was then tried for heresy and found guilty. He was executed in 1536, first by being hung and then by being burned. Ironically, the English version that drew heavily upon his work was in circulation in England with the king's permission a few months before his death, but word did not reach his captors on the continent of Europe in time to halt his execution.

The Coverdale Bible

Miles Coverdale not only produced the Coverdale Bible in 1535, but he also had a part in editing the Great Bible of 1539 and in preparing the Geneva Bible in 1560. He was an assistant to Tyndale on the continent for a while in the late

1520s. He was among many who felt that King Henry VIII approved of having an authorized translation for the people to read, so his Bible contains a flowery dedication to King Henry. He never mentioned Tyndale by name, but was heavily dependent upon Tyndale's work. To mention Tyndale would have terminated his own efforts immediately. He used Tyndale's New Testament and his Pentateuch and Jonah translations. To these he added the rest of the Old Testament based on his translations from Latin and German, the latter of which he called 'Dutch'. Not being a scholar in the Hebrew and Greek languages, that was his only option. He also revised Tyndale's New Testament in light of the German. In his Bible, Coverdale was the first to separate the books of the Apocrypha from the rest of the Old Testament books and print them separately at the end of the Old Testament, thus setting a pattern for subsequent English versions.

To Coverdale belonged the distinction of producing the first complete, printed English Bible based for the most part on Hebrew and Greek. It was printed on the Continent and imported into England. His Bible did not play a major part in English life for long, however, though it was reprinted four times (1537 [twice], 1550, and 1553).

Matthew's Bible
The name of Matthew's Bible was based on the pen name 'Thomas Matthew', a name adopted by John Rogers, another of Tyndale's associates. He took that name to escape the fate that had befallen Tyndale. In spite of his use of a pen name, however, Rogers was burned at the stake as a Christian martyr in 1555.

Matthew's Bible was largely Tyndale's work supplemented by Coverdale's in portions of the Old Testament not completed by Tyndale. It was preferred over Coverdale's work, however, because it was closer to Tyndale's translation without the revisions made by Coverdale in the New Testament.

Thomas Cranmer urged the king to license this version, a request that was granted. At the same time the king also issued a license for Coverdale's second 1537 edition. Interestingly, two licensed versions were in free circulation in England the year after Tyndale's death.

The Great Bible

After the granting of official approval for the circulation of Bibles in English, the decision came to revise Matthew's Bible and make it more widely acceptable. One feature of Matthew's Bible that made it objectionable to some was its pointedly Protestant notes. The revision removed those notes and made other improvements deemed necessary. Miles Coverdale gave oversight to the task of revision, which began in May of 1538. Political developments held the work up, however, until April 1539. Thomas Cranmer wrote the preface for the revision, usually called 'The Great Bible', but sometimes referred to as 'Cranmer's Bible' because he wrote the preface. The basis for the work was Matthew's Bible rather than Coverdale's, because of the recognized superiority of the former.

The Bible in English continued in circulation for the next few years until Mary Tudor became Queen of England in 1553. She prohibited public reading of Scripture. Obviously she allowed no Bibles to be published in England during her reign.

The Geneva Bible

Several British reformers, including Miles Coverdale, John Knox, and William Whittingham, fled England because of the persecution of Queen Mary. In Geneva they found refuge under the protection of John Calvin, who exercised some authority there. The group, with Whittingham probably taking a leading part, produced the Geneva Bible in 1560. The work included a revision of the Old Testament so thorough that it could be considered a new translation. For this reason, it usually stands apart from the Tyndale tradition. The new translation was necessary because the books of the Old Testament not translated by Tyndale from Hebrew and Aramaic were for the first time put into English directly from the original languages. The basis of the translation in the New Testament was the 1534 edition of Tyndale. Books of the Apocrypha were translated, but a preface to them indicated that they were by common consent not received and were not to be read and expounded in the church.

The Geneva Bible achieved almost immediate recognition and a rapid popularity. Its popularity continued for some time, even after the translation of the version under King James' auspices. The Geneva Bible was the one used by William Shakespeare; it was also the first English Bible to have verse divisions. Its impact was so profound that Scripture quotations in the introduction to the King James Version derived from the Geneva Bible. The call for some 180 editions of the Geneva Bible, the last of them in 1644, attests the widespread popularity of the version.

The Bishops' Bible
With the Great Bible rapidly falling into disuse because of popular acceptance of the Geneva Bible, authorities within the Church of England determined that it was time for a revision of the Great Bible. The production of the Geneva Bible outside the country was one factor against its acceptance throughout Great Britain. In addition, its Calvinistic notes were unacceptable in England, although they were well received in Scotland, where Geneva had strongly influenced the Reformation movement. Because of

these negative factors, the Church of England decided upon a revision which was proposed in 1561, completed in 1568, and called the Bishops' Bible. The basis for the revision was the Great Bible of 1539. The parts of the Old Testament which had been translated from Latin in the Bible of 1539 were checked against the Hebrew text. The project was under the leadership of Archbishop Matthew Parker.

In spite of its intentions to the contrary, the Bishops' Bible was unable to stem the popularity of the Geneva Bible.

The King James Version

King James came to the throne of England in 1603. Early in 1604, at the famous Hampton Court Conference, he received a suggestion from the Puritan, John Reynolds. Reynolds proposed the need for a new translation acceptable to all parties. His intent in suggesting this was the removal of the High Church terminology used in the Bishops' Bible. King James acted upon his suggestion and appointed a group to undertake the revision project, but among the stipulations given to the translators was the instruction to retain the High Church terminology. It was well-known that King James had little use for the Puritan position.

Another guideline given the translators was to change the Bishops' Bible only when absolutely necessary. They were granted permission to adopt consensus renderings of other earlier translations, including the Great Bible and the Geneva Bible, whenever they felt it proper. Influence of the Rheims (i.e., Douai) New Testament is also visible in their work at times. Relatively speaking, however, their changes were minor in comparison with the total product. To illustrate how minor their changes were, it has been estimated that ninety to ninety-two percent of the King James New Testament is still the work of William Tyndale, even after revisions represented in Matthew's Bible, the Great Bible, and the Bishops' Bible.

James invited fifty-four scholars to participate in the revision effort. A few refused, and some were unable to participate because of health. Of the fifty who probably did participate, only forty-seven names are still available. The forty-seven divided into six groups, three dealing with the Old Testament, two with the New, and one with the Apocrypha. The assignments of the three Old Testament groups were Genesis to Kings, Chronicles to Song of Solomon, and Isaiah to Malachi. The first New Testament group was given the four Gospels, Acts, and Revelation, and the second group was responsible for the rest of the New Testament, the epistles.

The Old Testament. Of the ten men assigned to the first Old Testament committee, probably the best known was Lancelot Andrewes. Andrewes represented churchmanship at its best. He was an extremely accurate and painstaking scholar, the master of fifteen languages, a preacher of great power, with deep and mature personal piety. Recognizing his qualities, James appointed him to three bishoprics, the last in 1619 being an appointment to one of the oldest and richest in England. Frequent Greek and Latin quotations characterized Andrewes' sermons. His special ability in languages stemmed from his practice of learning a new language during each of his vacations. One of his contemporaries said of him that he could have qualified as the 'interpreter-general at Babel'. Like most of the other forty-seven translators, Andrewes never married.

Another member of the same company was John Overall. Overall never obtained the complete approval of the king because of his refusal to accept the Tudor conception of the divine right of kings that James espoused. Just before beginning the project, he married one of the most famous and beautiful women in England, whose subsequent conduct as his wife caused extensive gossip before the project was completed.

Another member of this same committee was Richard Thompson, a confirmed anti-Calvinist. He was widely renowned for his skill in languages, but he also had a terrible drinking problem. It was said of him that he never went to bed sober.

In contrast to the first Old Testament committee which met at Westminster and the third committee which met at Oxford, the second Old Testament committee met at Cambridge. An interesting member of this group of eight was Lawrence Chatterton, one of four Puritan leaders who had participated in the Hampton Court conference. While a student, he embraced the Puritan position. His Roman Catholic father tried to dissuade him by offering to care for all his needs if he would renounce Puritanism. Lawrence refused, so his father sent him a shilling to buy a beggar's wallet. Chatterton persevered, however, and continued to live a life of distinction. He became the first head of the Emmanuel College. He lived to age 103. Even at the end of his life he was able to read his Greek New Testament without glasses and to converse without the repetition that usually accompanies senility.

Another interesting member was Francis Billingham. His knowledge of Greek was so great that he used the Greek language in debates where Latin had been customary. He was a well-known male chauvinist, but vigorously defended the right of the clergy to marry. Though a confirmed bachelor, he wrote a marriage manual advising husbands how to retain control of their wives.

Another member of this second panel was John Richardson. Richardson was known for his excessive weight and for his rigorous anti-Calvinistic stand. He was also bold enough at one point to contend against King James that the church had the right to excommunicate kings.

John Reynolds was the most famous member of the third Old Testament group, composed of seven members. His suggestion at the Hampton Court conference led eventually to the launching of the project. He was a strong spokesman for Calvinism on the panel; he was also sympathetic toward Puritanism and championed it at the conference. He was very learned and possessed great quality of character that brought him high respect even from his enemies. He was a pious man and excelled in scholarship. He was prominent even though James had little use for Puritanism. Reynolds died in 1607 while the project was still in progress. His great devotion to the project may have hastened his death. He was famous as a Greek scholar and was as good a Hebraist as any of the translators.

A prominent member of the third panel was Thomas Holland, who died soon after completion of the project. He was one of the older members of the panel and was somewhat of a nonconformist in doctrine. Specifically, he did not accept that bishops were of a different order from elders. He was a pious man and learned in the church fathers. As he grew older, he gave more and more time to prayer.

Another well-known member of this third group was Miles Smith, an extreme Puritan. Though a Puritan, he received the distinction of writing the translators' preface to the new Bible. He was also distinguished in that he was one of the final editors of the Bible; along with one other, he put the finishing touches to it after the committees had completed all their work. Others gave a large amount of credit for the translation to him, but he refused to accept any credit for himself.

The New Testament. The first committee that worked on the New Testament had eight members. The chairman of the committee was Thomas Ravis. His antipathy toward Puritans was well-known. He felt that the strength of the Reformation in England depended on unity in principle as well as unity of practice, and so he looked upon the Puritans as a threat to that unity. He died in 1609, before completion of the translation, having earned a reputation for lavish spending on social affairs and for spending church funds on his own church properties.

George Abbot, another member of this first New Testament committee, was perhaps even better known than Ravis. His Puritan sympathies made him distasteful to the opposition party, the English church, but he found favor with James in 1606 by defending the king's views regarding the nature of kingship against Overall. In 1608 he was selected for a mission to Scotland to sell the Scots an Episcopal form of government. Against significant odds, Abbot was successful in his mission, and on the basis of his success, began receiving choice appointments by the king. At age sixty, while on a hunting trip, Abbot accidentally killed a gamekeeper with one of his arrows. Though accidental, the death deeply moved him to adopt a monthly fast for the rest of his life and to contribute liberally to the gamekeeper's widow. Though thoroughly penitent, he was still a man of blood and was thereby disqualified from serving the church. After a time of suspension, a commission of six bishops and four laymen heard his case. The commission was evenly divided on the issue of his future service. James cast a deciding vote in his favor, restoring him to his position. He was a man of great integrity, but also of fatherly tenderness. It was he who at the death of James crowned Charles I as James' successor.

A third interesting member of this first New Testament committee was Henry Seville. He was a great scholar, and after one of his scholarly research trips through Europe, he was appointed Greek tutor for Queen Elizabeth. He expended exorbitant amounts of time researching Saint Chrysostom, of whose works he was preparing a monumental edition. His wife resented bitterly all the time spent on this research, and on the occasion of an illness of her husband, threatened to burn his research, thinking that Chrysostom was killing him.

He finally published his work on Chrysostom, the first grand scale work of learning to be printed in England aside from the Bible. He went to great lengths to print this work, but it was a failure in the marketplace. He must have been a man of great wealth; otherwise he could not have afforded such a project.

The other New Testament committee, working on the epistles, was composed of seven members, no one of which was of particularly outstanding reputation.

The Apocrypha committee undertook their work with mixed emotions. The seven men who composed the committee were not assured that their work was worthwhile. An interesting member of this group was John Bois. He had been an extremely bright child with an ability to read the Hebrew Bible at age six. His diligence matched his brilliance. He began his studies at 4:00 in the morning and continued straight through until 8:00 at night. Initially he prepared for a career in medicine but subsequently decided that that field was not worthy enough. He turned to linguistics, which eventually led to his appointment to the translating team. Though personally he was a pleasant, humble, and entirely respected person, he had an unhappy marriage because of his wife's excessive spending habits. In addition to his work on the Apocrypha team, he also participated on the second Old Testament committee and was one of those who did the general revision at the end of the project. He kept the only notes on the committee discussions that have survived any of the companies. The notes, which were later translated from Latin, give interesting insights into the reasoning, scholarship, and method of the committees.

Another interesting member of the same group was Andrew Downes. An intensely aggressive person, he was a distinguished classicist and an expert on Demosthenes. He was an exceptionally intolerant and abrasive person who was very hard to get along with. He was known for his endless quarreling in committee work. His relations with the other translators grew worse when they found out that among all the translators, he alone had persuaded King James to pay him for his services. After the completion of the Apocrypha, Downes was transferred to the second New Testament committee, where he apparently made his influence felt very keenly. One feature of the New Testament translation which is probably attributable to his later appearance on the committee is the use of the English word 'charity' to translate the Greek ἀγάπη (*agapē*), beginning at 1 Corinthians 8:1 and continuing through the rest of the epistles. Translators rendered the word as 'love' in passages before 1 Corinthians 8.

One individual who did not serve on a translation committee but was appointed to help Miles Smith in the work of final revision was Thomas Bilson. He provided a summary statement at the head of each chapter and offered other types of general assistance in the final stages of the work.

Miscellaneous features. Reports of King James' personal habits of using bad language are a blemish on his character. Reportedly, the minutes of the Hampton Court conference that gave birth to the King James project had to be purged of all the expletives that came from the King's mouth. This purging guarded against offending the sensibilities of Christian readers. The probability is that James initiated the project to win for himself a place in history. James himself was somewhat of a scholar in his own right, but not on a level that would qualify him for active participation in the revision effort.

Other interesting features regarding the King James Version include the fact that it was the first Bible to make extensive use of both Jewish and Catholic scholarship in its production. Another interesting facet is that although it is often called the 'Authorized Version', no official act of authorization is on record anywhere. The immediate popularity of the King James Version after its completion was obvious. Its intrinsic superiority to anything done previously made itself felt very soon after publication. Three editions came during the first year of its availability. Not too many years later it overtook the Geneva Bible in popularity. One action that facilitated this was the termination of the printing of the Geneva Bible after 1644.

The need to which the King James Version responded is interesting. The famous Hampton Court conference in 1604 had as its purpose to determine what was wrong with the church. The only significant action of the conference was the following resolution: 'That a translation be made of the whole Bible, as consonant as can be to the original Hebrew and Greek; and this to be set out and printed, without any marginal notes, and only to be used in all Churches of England in time of divine service.' The resolution passed, but not unanimously. The king received the motion with great enthusiasm.

Aside from direct dependence of the project on the Bishop's Bible and its frequent reference to the Great Bible and Geneva Bible, the influence of the Rheims New Testament was also strong in the translation of the King James Version.

Revisions of the King James Version continued throughout the first 350 years of its existence. Some passages are still in bad need of revision. A modern printing of the King James Version has the expression 'straining at a gnat' (Matthew 23:24), whereas the 1611 edition correctly translates it 'straining *out* a gnat'. A further interesting detail is that the first Bible printed in the United States of America was the King James Version. In America however, during those early years, the Apocryphal books were never included as they were in Great Britain.

The English Revised Version

The changing nature of the English language and the growing availability of earlier New Testament manuscripts prompted the production of the English Revised Version of 1881 (New Testament) and 1885 (complete Bible). The latter cause made the four members of the translation team who were specialists in New Testament textual criticism of strategic importance to the project. The four were F. H. A. Scrivener, S. P. Tregelles, B. F. Westcott, and F. J. A. Hort. Of the four, Tregelles was unable to take an active part because of poor health. Scrivener leaned toward favoring the 'Received Text' or the *Textus Receptus*. Westcott and Hort vigorously supported what they called a Neutral text (more recently referred to as an Alexandrian text) that is best represented in two manuscripts called Vaticanus and Sinaiticus. The two men were in process of producing their own critical Greek text, a publication that appeared five days before the English Revised Version New Testament. Since the two constituted a majority of the active committee, their decisions determined the Greek text translated in the English Revised Version New Testament.

The position of Westcott and Hort on this issue came under vigorous attack from Dean Burgon, who was an avid, passionate supporter of the traditional text that had constituted the basis of English translations of the New Testament up to that time.

Three earlier translation-related works set the tone for the ERV: an interim report by Dean Alford in 1869, John Nelson Darby's New Translation of the New Testament in 1871 and Old Testament in 1890, and Robert Young's literal translation in 1862. In 1870 an ecclesiastical committee of the Church of England initiated the English Revised Version project with five resolutions:

(1) That it is desirable that a revision of the Authorized Version of the Holy Scriptures be undertaken;

(2) That the revision be so conducted as to comprise both marginal renderings and such emendations as it may be found necessary to insert in the text of the Authorized Version;

(3) That in the above resolutions we do not contemplate any new translation of the Bible or any alteration of the language except when in the judgment of the most competent scholars such change is necessary;

(4) That in such necessary changes, the style of the language employed in the existing version be closely followed;

(5) That it is desirable that the convocation should nominate a body of its own members to undertake the work of revision. They shall be at liberty to invite the cooperation of any well-known scholar, no matter what nation or religious body he may belong to.

General principles to be followed by the revisers included a directive to alter the Authorized Version as few times as possible and a directive to adopt a text for which the evidence is decidedly preponderating, with alterations to the Authorized Version indicated in the margin whenever they occur.

An attempt to incorporate American scholarship into the project proved fruitless because of differences in the English spoken on the two sides of the Atlantic, so the American counterpart, the American Standard Version (ASV), appeared in 1901, sixteen years after the complete Bible of the English Revised Version. The appendix of the British edition contained American-preferred readings, and the American edition printed British-preferred readings in its appendix.

The Revised Standard Version

After World War I, in 1928, the copyright for the American Standard Version became the property of the International Council of Religious Education, now the Department of

Christian Education of the National Council of Churches of Christ in the United States and Canada. An intent to revise the American Standard Version surfaced, but the Depression of the early 1930s delayed the beginning of the project somewhat. Such a revision finally received authorization in 1937, with the stated purpose to 'embody the best results of modern scholarship as to the meaning of the Scriptures, and express this meaning in English diction which is designed for use in public and private worship and preserves those qualities which have given to the King James Version a supreme place in English literature'.

Thirty-two scholars received appointments as committee members. They came from several backgrounds. Their expertise was in academic areas related to the original languages and in English, and in experience with conducting public worship. The committee members received no stipends or honorariums; rather, they contributed their time and energies for the good of the cause. They were divided into two sections, one to deal with the Old Testament and the other with the New. The New Testament appeared in 1946 and the whole Bible in 1952. At the time of the publication of the complete Bible, three thousand religious services were held simultaneously across the United States.

The Revised Standard Version translators did not attempt a new translation but a revision. The result of their work, however, is a more thorough revision than was the American Standard Version. Nevertheless the work still conforms to the general pattern and sometimes the exact wording of Tyndale's work. The translators sought to make a good translation better, as had the producers of the King James Version.

Meetings of the ongoing revision committee were held in 1954, 1959, 1965, 1968, and 1970. More recently, a meeting has been held every year. Though produced by American scholars, the work has also been favorably received among British readers. When the Revised Standard Version came out as the text of the Oxford Annotated Bible in 1962, it was the first Protestant annotated edition to receive official approval for study by the Roman Catholic Church. A Catholic edition of the RSV New Testament came in 1965 and one of the whole Bible in 1966. The Common Bible was released in 1973. It is an ecumenical edition of the Revised Standard Version which supercedes the need for separate Catholic and Protestant editions. It also has the blessing of the Eastern Orthodox Church. An enlarged work became available in 1976, including additional apocryphal books accepted by certain Eastern Orthodox churches. The expanded edition of the New Oxford Annotated Bible with the Apocrypha was published on May 19, 1977, marking the first time since the Reformation that one edition of the Bible has the blessing of leaders of the Protestant, Roman Catholic, and Eastern Orthodox churches alike.

The New American Standard Bible
The New American Standard Bible New Testament appeared in 1963 and the entire Bible in 1971. It was a revision and modernization of the American Standard Version of 1901, as was the Revised Standard Version, but the translators held a more conservative theological viewpoint than those of the Revised Standard Version. One purpose of the NASB was to revive interest in the fast-disappearing American Standard Version.

The principles of the Lockman Foundation originally did not allow a naming of the editorial board members, but the names have since been divulged. All members subscribed to the conservative theological statement of the Foundation. The intention was that the translation stand on its own merit and that the glory for whatever is beneficial in it be given to Christ.

Sixty-eight scholars and pastors participated in the project. They came from a number of different denominational backgrounds: Presbyterian, Methodist, Southern Baptist, Church of Christ, Nazarene, American Baptist, Independent Fundamental Churches of America, Conservative Baptist, Free Methodist, Congregational, Disciples of Christ, Evangelical Free, General Association of Regular Baptists, Independent Baptist, Independent Mennonite, Assemblies of God, North American Baptist, and others. Chairman of the editorial board throughout the project was Reuben Olson.

In common with other translations, the goals were to be true to the original, grammatically correct, and understandable to the masses.

The New King James Version
Thomas Nelson, Incorporated – particularly its present president, Sam Moore – initiated the New King James Version project. Moore conceived of the project in response to his son's request for a Bible he could understand. The New Testament was published in 1979 and the Old Testament in 1982. The cost of the project was 3.5 million dollars.

The NKJV is viewed by its producers as a new and improved edition of the old King James Version. Actually the old King James Version underwent many revisions after its initial publication. The edition of 1769, which became the standard of the King James Version used today, differed from the 1611 edition in an estimated 75,000 details. A comparison of the NKJV with Jay Green's Modern King James Version, released in 1962, shows the two to be very close to each other, much closer than the NKJV is to the original King James Version.

The 119 translators came from several denominational groups, including Methodist, Baptist, Presbyterian, Lutheran, Assemblies of God, Nazarene, Churches of Christ, and others.

The New Revised Standard Version

In 1974 the National Council of Churches of Christ authorized work that led to the appearance of the New Revised Standard Version in 1989. The revisers concentrated their efforts in three areas:

(1) less formality in social relationships, including the elimination of the 'thee's and 'thou's in speech addressed to God;

(2) the elimination of 'sex-biased' language by incorporating inclusivist language, though the version has retained masculine terms for God;

(3) a loosening of traditional constraints to retain some familiar King James Version phrases.

The NRSV has retained from the Revised Standard Version the same theological problems that have made the version of limited usefulness to those holding conservative doctrine (see chapter 4 of this work). In addition, its effort to incorporate inclusivist language has made it a considerably less literal translation than is the RSV (see chapter 3 of this work).

The New American Standard Bible Updated

In 1995 the Lockman Foundation released an updated edition of the New American Standard Bible. Their purpose in doing so was to increase the clarity and readability of the NASB. The vocabulary, grammar, and sentence structure underwent minor revisions to provide for smoother reading. In conjunction with releasing the updated edition, the Foundation also for the first time released the names of all participants in translating the original NASB and the updated edition.

Since it first appeared in 1963 and 1971, the chief distinguishing feature of the NASB, the one that has captured most attention, has been its word-for-word correspondence with the original languages of Scripture where the English language would allow for it. In its effort to attain greater smoothness in style, the updated edition has to a degree surrendered that unique feature. In other words, the updated edition is not as literal a translation as the original NASB (see chapter 3 of this work).

The schema found on the next page shows the translations of the Tyndale tradition and their relationships to one another.

ENGLISH TRANSLATIONS OUTSIDE THE TYNDALE TRADITION

In the strictest sense, no other 'traditions' of English translations exist because of the sparsity of history behind almost all the rest of the translations. Nevertheless, knowing about the genesis of other translations is beneficial.

The Douai Bible (1582, 1609-10)

An exception to the 'no tradition' generalization is the Douai Bible that English Roman Catholics in exile from their home country translated at Douai in northern France. The principal translator of the work was Gregory Martin. He published the New Testament in 1582 and the Old Testament in 1609-10.

The Douai Bible stood in the tradition of Wycliffe because Martin based his work on the Latin Vulgate, the official version of the Roman Catholic Church since the Council of Trent (1546). He scrupulously followed the Latin to the extent that the English at certain points is incomprehensible. He did consult the Hebrew and Greek at times, because Latin has no definite article, one particular in which this translation is superior to the King James Version. His work exercised general influence over the King James Version translators in the production of that version.

The work contained a very full set of annotations in support

The Tyndale Tradition of Translations

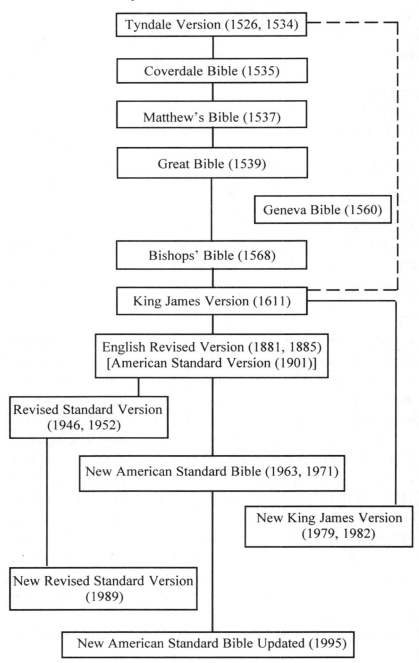

of the doctrines of Roman Catholicism. Richard Challoner published five revisions of the New Testament and two of the Old Testament between 1749 and 1772 with a view to making the English more intelligible. Some of the renderings of the King James Version influenced him because of his earlier years spent as a Protestant under the influence of the 1611 work. In 1810 the Douai Bible became authorized for Roman Catholics in America, a status it held almost exclusively among English translations until well into the twentieth century.

The Confraternity Version (New American Bible) (1941, 1970)

A revision of the Douai New Testament, also called the Rheims-Challoner New Testament, was published in 1941. Scholars belonging to the Catholic Biblical Association of America did the work. The Episcopal Confraternity of Christian Doctrine sponsored the project, hence the name the Confraternity Version. It was, of course, based on the Latin Vulgate like its predecessor.

The Old Testament of this version came in four stages: 1952, 1955, 1961, and 1969. Its basis, however, was the Hebrew rather than the Latin Vulgate Old Testament. The decision to use the Hebrew came, of course, after a Vatican Council in the 1950s allowed Roman Catholic scholars to begin using the Hebrew and Greek rather than the Latin in their scholarly pursuits.

Since it was not fitting to have an Old Testament based on the Hebrew text bound with a New Testament based on the Latin, the translators prepared a revision of the New Testament based on the Greek original, and in 1970 presented it with a slightly revised Old Testament under a new title of the New American Bible. Fifty-nine Catholic scholars worked on the project, but toward the end several Protestant scholars also participated as translators and editors. The new name reflects the more ecumenical character of the revised work.

At this point the work ceased to be a revision of the Douai Bible and assumed the proportions of a new translation, devoid of a lengthy historical lineage.

The Twentieth Century New Testament (1901)

The first in a long series of 'modern English' translations was the Twentieth Century New Testament. It first appeared in 1901, but the permanent edition did not come until 1904. The purpose of the work was to make the Bible clear for the sake of young people and the uneducated.

Participants in the project remained anonymous for over fifty years after the translation's completion, but now twenty men and women who worked for fourteen years to complete it have been identified. These translators shared the common trait of being somewhat radical in their outlook regarding social and religious matters. They were not linguists, but they claimed their work was based on the Greek text recommended by Westcott and Hort. To their credit, they consulted reputable linguists such as Richard Francis Weymouth from time to time. Their collaboration with one another was entirely by mail since they were never able to meet together as a group.

Moody Press reprinted an edition of the volume in 1961. The Twentieth Century New Testament deserves inclusion in this discussion because it 'broke the ice' for a free translation movement that has become widespread during the latter half of the twentieth century.

The New Testament in Modern Speech (1903)

Richard Francis Weymouth did a translation of his own, based on his work The Resultant Greek Testament (1862), and called it The New Testament in Modern Speech. The Greek text followed was that agreed upon by a majority of nineteenth century editors whose special interest was a study of the text.

His work appeared in 1903, after Weymouth had died, with Ernest Hampden-Cook, a Congregationalist minister and one of the Twentieth Century New Testament translators, adding the final touches. This was a high quality translation, a modern English translation as the title reflects. It had a better scholarly basis than the Twentieth Century New Testament, however. It was reprinted frequently, and in 1924 James Alexander Robertson thoroughly revised it. In that edition some of Weymouth's unorthodox doctrinal biases were eliminated (see chapter 4 of this work).

A New Translation of the Bible (1913, 1926)

In 1913 James Moffatt published The New Testament: A New Translation and in 1924 he published The Old Testament: A New Translation. The complete Bible, called A New Translation of the Bible, came in 1926.

Moffatt was a brilliant Scottish scholar who specialized in New Testament studies. He was a genius in capturing his interpretations of Scripture in vivid, contemporary Scottish idiom. He served from 1915 to 1927 as professor of Church History at the United Free College at Glasgow and from 1927 to 1939 at Union Theological Seminary in New York City. During this last period he served on the committee that produced the Revised Standard Version.

The Complete Bible: An American Translation (1927, 1931)

Edgar J. Goodspeed, a widely acknowledged New Testament scholar during the first half of the twentieth century, voiced public criticisms of the Twentieth Century New Testament and of the translations of Weymouth and Moffatt, and then produced a translation that did not have the weaknesses he perceived. One of his criticisms was that Americans had for too long been dependent on versions produced across the Atlantic, so he, an American scholar, produced one for Americans.

His work proved to be an apt counterpart to Moffatt's work in Scotland. With the release of his New Testament in 1927 and a revision of the same in 1935, Goodspeed proved his ability at incorporating American idioms in a free translation. In 1931 J. M. Powis Smith combined Goodspeed's New Testament with an Old Testament translation into a complete Bible. Goodspeed translated the Apocrypha and included it in the 1939 edition.

Goodspeed joined Moffatt in serving among those who comprised the New Testament committee that produced the RSV.

The New Testament in the Language of the People (1937)

The New Testament in the Language of the People, the work of Charles B. Williams, first appeared in the United States in 1937. A unique feature of this version is its attempt to show in its English renderings the various tense nuances of the Greek verb. That makes for very interesting reading for a person with facility in the Greek language, but for most readers the translation is too cumbersome. Stretching out verb meanings to such lengths creates English that is uneven and very difficult to read in a normal fashion.

The Knox Translation (1945, 1949)

Ronald A. Knox translated an official version of the Bible for Roman Catholics based on the Latin Vulgate. The New Testament came in 1945 and the Old Testament in 1949. He consulted the original Hebrew and Greek, but the Clementine Vulgate, the standard for the Roman Catholic Church since

1592, was the authoritative basis for the translation.

Knox's ability in English expression was notable. He was a master at obtaining 'equivalent effect' upon the English reader in comparison with the earliest readers of the text. His rendering of the Song of Songs is probably the most beautiful translation of this portion in the English language.

A Roman Catholic theological bias is quite evident in the work. Extensive notes, especially in the New Testament, sometimes clarify the text, but sometimes they defend Roman Catholic doctrine.

The Bible in Basic English (1940, 1949)

S. H. Hooke translated the Bible into English utilizing C. K. Ogden's vocabulary of 850 words through which a person could allegedly give the sense of anything that could be said in English. The use of such a basic vocabulary catered to the needs of people whose first language was not English. The New Testament of The Bible in Basic English appeared in 1940, and the whole Bible in 1949.

The Holy Bible: The Berkeley Version in Modern English (The Modern Language Bible) (1945, 1959)

In 1945 Gerrit Verkuyl published the New Testament of the Berkeley Version and called upon twenty scholars for help in translating the Old Testament of The Holy Bible: The Berkeley Version in Modern English. The complete Bible became available in 1959. Verkuyl saw the version, named after the Californian city where he did most of his work on the New Testament, as a theologically conservative counterpart to the Revised Standard Version.

Zondervan Publising House released a revised edition of the work in 1969, at which time it received the name Modern Language Bible.

The New Testament in Modern English (1947-1957)

J. B. Phillips began paraphrasing the New Testament letters amid the duress of World War II in England. He purposed to provide encouragement to his fellow Englishmen during those dark days. After reading the rendition of his first book, C. S. Lewis urged him to continue with the rest of the New Testament.

He issued Letters to Young Churches in 1947, followed by The Gospels in Modern English in 1952. The Young Church in Action, his paraphrase of the book of Acts, came in 1955 and The Book of Revelation in 1957.

In 1973 Phillips published a translation of the Old Testament books of Amos, Hosea, Isaiah 1–35, and Micah. He did not complete the Old Testament, however. He had a limited knowledge of the Hebrew language and encountered many difficulties in his Old Testament work.

He produced a revision of the New Testament in 1973. Two goals marked this revision. He wanted to update the idiom of the 1940s and to make his renderings a little more literal. By this time people had begun using his work for Bible study purposes, viewing the work as authoritative. That was a use which Phillips had not originally envisioned, so he tried to restrict some of the extreme freedom of his renderings.

The New World Translation (1950, 1961)

The Watchtower Bible and Tract Society, Inc., translated and in 1950 released the New World Translation of the Christian Greek Scriptures. The counterpart New World Translation of the Hebrew Scriptures came in 1961 when the whole Bible appeared. The organization has also released two more editions (1970 and 1971).

As would be expected, the translation displays the unorthodox theological tendencies that are associated with the Jehovah's Witness movement.

The New Testament: A New Translation in Plain English (1952)

Charles Kingsley Williams was experienced in working with people whose first language was not English, but who needed English for purposes of higher education. Using a basic English vocabulary of 1,500 words contained in the Interim Report on Vocabulary Selection (London, 1936), he prepared and in 1952 circulated The New Testament: A New Translation in Plain English. He did not limit himself strictly to the list of 1,500, but added between 160 and 170 more words that he explained in a glossary at the end of the volume. The work has the advantage of a larger list of words, particularly verbs, to draw from than the earlier Basic English Version.

Expanded Translation of the New Testament (1956-1959)

Kenneth S. Wuest, a long-time professor at the Moody Bible Institute, followed in the train of Charles B. Williams. He sought to bring nuances of the Greek original over into the English translation more so than had been done previously. Whereas Williams limited his attention to Greek verbs, Wuest included the rest of the parts of speech too. This made for an interesting and at points helpful study tool, but his translation had too many embellishments to allow for normal reading. This work originally appeared in three volumes between 1956 and 1959.

The Amplified Bible (1958, 1965)

The leading figure in the preparation of the Amplified Bible was Frances E. Siewert, the wife of a Presbyterian minister who herself had training at Princeton Seminary along with her husband. She undertook her work on the New Testament under the sponsorship of The Lockman Foundation, and Zondervan Publishing House published her New Testament in 1958. The New Testament was such a glowing success in the marketplace that Zondervan engaged Mrs Siewert to proceed with work on the Old Testament. Part 2 of the Old Testament appeared in 1962, and Part 1 in 1964. The Amplified Bible became available in 1965, the Editorial Board of The Lockman Foundation having made extensive revisions to the earlier two-part Old Testament.

The Amplified Bible is even more expansive in its renderings than Wuest's work. In addition, it has alternative renderings which are more than expansions. They are renderings that in some cases reflect conflicting interpretations of the same passage.

The New English Bible (1961, 1970)
Just before World War II, a movement in Great Britain was afoot to revise the Revised Version of 1885, but the disruption caused by the war halted progress on that effort. A parallel effort in the United States to revise the American Standard Version of 1901 continued through the war years without interruption, however, the New Testament being completed in 1946. After the war the British group sensed that it was futile to continue their project in that same direction, realizing that it would but duplicate, for the most part, what had now been completed in America, so they adopted a different approach.

The question was raised as to whether successive revisions of earlier versions was meeting the needs of the present day. The group adopted a suggestion that a completely new translation be made. The idea originated in the General Assembly of the Church of Scotland which then invited the Church of England and the principal Free Churches of the British Isles to join them in the project. Thus began, in post World War II years, the first official fresh translation into English (the King James Version was not a fresh translation and the Tyndale Version was not official). It is a legitimately 'authorized' version because it was produced by leading Protestant churches of Great Britain and therefore possesses an authority and a status that no private translation has.

Four panels of scholars involved themselves in the project, one for the Old Testament, one for the Apocrypha, one for the New Testament, and one to advise on English literary and stylistic matters. The existence of this fourth panel accounts for the higher priority given to effective communication with contemporary society, an area in which the work of the Revised Standard Version had been criticized.

The year 1961 marked the arrival of the New Testament, published jointly by Oxford and Cambridge University Presses. It was an immediate best-seller, largely because of great sums of money spent on publicity. The complete New English Bible appeared in March of 1970.

The Revised English Bible (1989)

The Revised English Bible, a revision of the New English Bible, appeared in 1989. The REB differs in several respects from the NEB. Its translators strived to reduce the British idioms of the NEB so as to give the REB more of an international appeal. Instead of using an eclectic Greek text as its basis, the REB followed the text of the 1979 Nestle-Aland Novum Testamentum Graece. Also, the REB sought to utilize gender-inclusive language in contrast to the NEB, an objective that it achieved only partially. One of its major observable weaknesses is its inconsistency in this last regard.

The Good News Bible (Today's English Version) (1966, 1976)

The American Bible Society published the Good News Bible (earlier known as Today's English Version) New Testament in 1966. It was the showpiece for a philosophy of translation called 'dynamic equivalence', developed by Eugene Nida, the organization's leading translation scholar. A statement of this philosophy in Nida's 1964 work, *Toward a Science of Translation*, indicates it is an attempt to provide a theoretical basis for what had already been done in many English translations for over fifty years.

The leading figure in the translation was Robert G. Bratcher, a staff translator of the American Bible Society. He personally translated the New Testament, and chaired a committee of seven scholars who took eight years to complete the Old Testament. Second and third editions of the New Testament came in 1967 and 1971. The fourth edition of the New Testament joined with the newly completed Old Testament to comprise a complete Bible in 1976.

The work has circulated widely, to some extent because of the subsidized basis on which it has been available.

The Contemporary English Version (1991, 1995)
The CEV was an attempt to update the language of the Good News Bible to what people in the 1990s were accustomed to reading and hearing. Public reading was a primary concern of the translators. The version tried to incorporate gender-inclusive language except in references to God, and to avoid theological terms that would not be comprehensible to people without a biblical or theological background. The basis of the translation was the United Bible Societies' Biblia Hebraica Stuttgartensia in the Old Testament and Greek New Testament (third edition) in the New Testament, but the dynamic-equivalence translation philosophy followed obscures the degree of faithfulness to the original text that the version attained.

The Jerusalem Bible (1967)

The Jerusalem Bible is the English counterpart of La Bible de Jerusalem, a French translation that appeared in its abridged and simplified form in 1956. The English work was published in 1967. Introductions and notes are translations from the French, but the basis for biblical text is the Hebrew, Aramaic, and Greek originals. This was the first Catholic Bible to be translated from the original languages in its entirety. The work carries the *imprimatur* of the Roman Catholic Church.

Though Catholic scholars did the translating, they designed the JB for Bible readers in general. The translators were ecumenically minded Dominicans of the Dominican Biblical School of Jerusalem. Their notes are not as concerned with affirming traditional interpretations of Roman Catholicism as they are with clarifying the meaning of the text.

This is one of few modern versions that chose to render the personal name of God in the Old Testament by 'Yahweh' in English. The book introductions and notes reflect the opinions of current critical scholarship.

The New Jerusalem Bible (1986)

Criticisms of the freeness of translation policy in the Jerusalem Bible prompted a thorough revision, the name given the revision being The New Jerusalem Bible. Like the JB, the NJB is a study Bible with introductory and explanatory notes to facilitate understanding. The notes reflect the NJB's target audience of Catholic readers, as does the inclusion of books of the Apocrypha.

Though designed as a more literal descendant of the JB, the NJB at times reflects more affinity for modern English idiom than it does for accuracy in translating the original text. That tendency leaves the NJB open to the same criticism lodged against the JB, that of interpreting rather than translating. It also has consciously sought to incorporate gender-inclusive language in most areas, but not in referring to God as female or in translating the Greek ἀδελφοί (*adelphoi*) as 'brothers and sisters' rather than 'brothers'.

The Living Bible (1971)

Kenneth N. Taylor, working alone, produced the Living Bible. He used the American Standard Version of 1901 as the basis for his work, a project that resulted from his efforts to explain the meaning of the Bible to his ten children in everyday English they could understand. Taylor did a good part of the work on a commuter train between Chicago and Wheaton, Illinois.

Taylor, a conservative evangelical Christian, founded the Tyndale Publishing Company which published the Living Bible in the US (in Great Britain Kingsway Publications was the publisher). After special publicity provided the work by Billy Graham, the Living Bible became the best-selling book in the United States in 1972. In 1974 it accounted for 46% of Bible sales in the USA.

The work has been especially popular with young people. In its earlier years it carried the subtitle 'Paraphrase' on its title page, a designation that was subsequently dropped as the connotation of the word 'translation' broadened in many circles. Scholars of the American Bible Society, for example, consider its approach to be perfectly legitimate translation methodology and not at all paraphrastic.

The New Living Translation (1996)

The New Living Translation is a 1996 revision and updating of the Living Bible accomplished by checking the original Living Bible against the original languages of Scripture – the Masoretic Text of the Biblia Hebraica Stuttgartensia of 1977 in the Old Testament and the 1993 editions of the United

Bible Societies' Greek New Testament and of the Nestle-Aland Novum Testamentum Graece. The other goal of the ninety translators was to produce a new dynamic-equivalence translation that could stand on its own merits. The translation team came from an assortment of evangelical and Protestant seminaries and colleges in the USA, England, and Australia.

One marked difference between the Living Bible and the New Living Translation is the latter's consistent use of gender-neutral terminology. In a number of instances the New Living Translation has returned to more traditional renderings, such as in Psalm 23:1, 'The Lord is my shepherd', and in Genesis 1:1, 'In the beginning God created the heavens and the earth.' Translators geared the English of the New Living Translation to a sixth-grade reading level, which is considerably higher than the level of other contemporary English translations.

The New International Version (A Contemporary Translation) (1973, 1978)

The New York Bible Society undertook the sponsorship of an evangelical translation effort by 110 scholars from a number of different English-speaking countries, including the United States, Canada, England, Ireland, Scotland, Australia, and New Zealand. Earlier in the process, the name applied was A Contemporary Translation, but this was changed to the New International Version to reflect the multi-nation background and purpose of the project.

The beginning of the work dates back to 1956 when the Christian Reformed Church appointed a committee to study the feasibility of such a new translation. The National Association of Evangelicals did the same in 1957. The two efforts eventually merged and the New York Bible Society accepted leadership responsibility in 1967, appointing fifteen scholars to direct the work. In 1968 Edwin H. Palmer became full-time Executive Secretary of the project and the work began.

The New Testament came in 1973, and the whole Bible in 1978 was the first edition of the Old Testament alongside a freshly revised New Testament. In granting generous support to the Bible Society for the project, Zondervan obtained a 30-year exclusive right to publish the NIV. Hodder and Stoughton published an anglicized edition of the New Testament in 1974. The first edition of the NIV complete Bible was the largest printing ever done for an English Bible. Anticipation of widespread acceptance was great because of the unparalleled publicity given to the work.

The NIV is not a revision of an earlier translation, but according to its preface it has 'sought to preserve some measure of continuity with the long tradition of translating the Scriptures into English' (p. viii of its Introduction). The translators split into twenty teams with a translator, co-translator, two consultants, and an English stylist assigned to each team. The goal of the work, as has been that of many other similar efforts, was to replace the King James Version as the standard among conservative evangelicals, if not among all Christians.

The New International Reader's Version (1995)

This version, based on the NIV and abbreviated NIrV, sought to appeal to those with a limited literacy in English, being geared for children below the age of eight, for adults who read at or below the fourth-grade level, and for a growing number of people for whom English is a second language. Its textual basis (see chapter 2) is the same as for the NIV, but its translation technique (see chapter 3) displays more freedom in its attempt to simplify the text.

The New Century Version (1991)

Sponsored by Word Publishing Company, the New Century Version developed from an earlier translation, the International Children's Bible (New Testament in 1983, Old Testament in 1986). Like the ICB, the NCV used a vocabulary limited to words found in the *Living Word Vocabulary*, a guide used in preparation of *World Book Encyclopedia*. Most of the translators came from a broad theological range of evangelical seminaries and colleges.

The translation substituted modern equivalents for currency, weights, and measures. It retained the policy of ICB in using short sentences, and sought to update the meanings of English words that have in recent years undergone changes. The NCV translators also tried to use gender-inclusive language.

The Message (1993)

In 1993 NavPress issued The Message, a translation of the New Testament, Psalms, and Proverbs by Eugene Peterson, a Presbyterian pastor. Peterson reasoned that the informal nature of Greek in the New Testament required a translation in everyday English such as that used in discussing current events or in other types of informal personal conversations.

The Message is a paraphrase, meaning that many renderings are Peterson's own interpretations rather that what the Greek text says. It does capture current idiomatic 'street language' frequently, but often it does so at the expense of accuracy. Its 'catchy' language appeals to the casual or popular reader, but it does not stand up under the scrutiny of close study.

New English Translation

The New Testament of the New English Translation – also called the NET Bible – appeared in 1996-1998. The Biblical

Studies Press made a translation of the entire Bible available on an internet website free of charge. The Project Director, Translators, Editors, and Sponsors of the work remain unnamed in the published New Testament. The New Testament portion has 16,025 translators' footnotes that comment on textual critical matters, translators notes, and study notes of various types. The translation is of a dynamic-equivalence type with literal renderings often placed in the footnotes.

A chart on the following two pages lists translations outside the Tyndale tradition with their dates and with their revised editions, if any.

HISTORICAL SUMMARY

Remarks above reflect the existence of only one historical lineage of appreciable length, the one begun by William Tyndale in the sixteenth century. The remainder of the translations had interesting beginnings, but their historical roots are, relatively speaking, very shallow. The first decision we should face in choosing an English Bible translation is whether or not we want the translation to be one with a significant background in tradition or not. A translation with deep roots has profited from improvements made over a long period of time. That kind of growth provides a degree of stability and reliability. On the other hand, having an absolutely new translation could add freshness to our reading of Scripture. Each person must choose between the two options.

TRANSLATIONS OUTSIDE
THE TYNDALE TRADITION

Translation Name	Date	Revision Name	Date
Douai Bible	1582, 1609-10	*Rheims-Challoner New Testament*	1941
Confraternity Version (New American Bible)	1941, 1970		
Twentieth Century New Testament	1901		
New Testament in Modern Speech	1903		
New Translation of the Bible	1913 1926		
Complete Bible: An American Translation	1927 1931		
New Testament in the Language of the People	1937		
Knox Translation	1945, 1949		
Bible in Basic English	1940, 1949		
Holy Bible: The Berkeley Version in Modern English (Modern Language Bible)	1945, 1959		
New World Translation	1950, 1961		
New Testament: A New Translation in Plain English	1952		
Expanded Translation of the New Testament	1956-1959		
Amplified Bible	1958, 1965		

Translation Name	Date	Revision Name	Date
New English Bible	1961, 1970	*Revised English Bible*	1989
Good News Bible (Today's English Version)	1966, 1976	*Contemporary English Version*	1991, 1995
Jerusalem Bible	1967	*New Jerusalem Bible*	1986
Living Bible	1971	*New Living Translation*	1996
New International Version (A Contemporary Translation)	1973, 1978	*New International Reader's Version*	1995
New Century Version	1991		
The Message	1993		
New English Translation (NET Bible)	1996-1998		

Selected Reading List

Bratcher, Robert G. "Englishing the Bible," *Review and Expositor* 26/3 (Summer 1979): 299-314.

Bullard, Roger A. "Zeal to Promote the Common Good," *The Word of God: A Guide to English Versions of the Bible*. Lloyd R. Bailey, ed.; Atlanta: John Knox, 1982. 183-196.

Bruce, F. F. *History of the Bible in English*. 3rd ed.; New York: Oxford, 1978.

Goodspeed, Edgar J. *How Came the Bible*. New York: Abingdon-Cokesbury, 1940.

Greenslade, S. L. (ed.). *The Cambridge History of the Bible*. Cambridge: Cambridge University, 1963. 141-174, 361-382.

Kenyon, Sir Frederic. *Our Bible and the Ancient Manuscripts*. New York: Harper and Brothers, 1958. 265-320.

Kubo, Sakae, and Walter F. Specht. *So Many Versions?*. Revised Edition. Grand Rapids: Zondervan, 1983.

Lampe, G. W. H. (ed.). *The Cambridge History of the Bible*. Cambridge: Cambridge University, 1969. 362-414.

Lewis, Jack P. *The English Bible from KJV to NIV: A History and Evaluation*. 2nd ed. Grand Rapids: Baker, 1991.

Lightfoot, Neil R. *How We Got the Bible*. Grand Rapids: Baker, 1963. 96-105.

MacGregor, Geddes. *The Bible in the Making*. Philadelphia: J. B. Lippincott, 1959. 114-274.

MacGregor, Geddes. *A Literary History of the Bible*. Nashville: Abingdon, 1968.

Pollard, Alfred W. (ed.). *Records of the English Bible*. London: Oxford University, 1911.

Sheeley, Steven M., and Robert N. Hash, Jr. *The Bible in English Translation: An Essential Guide*. Nashville, Tenn.: Abingdon, 1997.

Weigle, Luther A. *The English New Testament from Tyndale to the Revised Standard Version*. New York: Abingdon, 1949.

Westcott, Brooke Foss. *A General View of the History of the English Bible*. New York: Macmillan, 1927.

Chapter 2

TEXTUAL BASES OF BIBLE TRANSLATIONS

A good bit of the confusion that exists regarding English translations of the Bible relates to the substance of the text's content in the original languages, the substance as distinguished from the various methods of expressing that substance. The average reader has difficulty explaining why two versions, in translating the same verse, differ in content so radically from each other. The answer to this dilemma often lies in an examination of the original text on which each bases its translation. Manuscript sources do not always agree with each other, and the English that renders those sources may reflect the disagreements.

An obviously crucial factor in Bible translation is the genuineness of the text translated. Variations exist in copies of the Old and New Testaments that have been preserved down to the present. The works that came from the authors of Bible books (or from their amanuenses or secretaries) are the ones that the Holy Spirit inspired, but when various scribes made copies from the original productions, changes gradually crept in. Scribes made some of these changes consciously, thinking they were correcting an earlier copying error, but they made most of them unconsciously. Whatever the cause, the fact remains that the modern translator has to decide between various readings in the text that he translates.

The task of recognizing which variations resulted from changes and which ones represent the inspired text is not a simple one. It is less complex for the Old Testament than for the New. For the Old fewer source documents are still available for analysis. In the New, however, an overwhelming proliferation of copies has posed a challenge to some of the best minds. Sifting through various possible wordings in each passage, to settle which is the one written initially from which all the others were derived, is a very complex task.

Families or Text-Types of Manuscripts

In the process of examining sources to establish the true original Greek text of the New Testament, an interesting feature emerges. The differing readings tend to group themselves into 'families' or 'text-types' in accordance with the way the sources agree with each other. 'Agree' means that in numbers of passages where manuscript sources retain different readings, manuscripts of the same text-type will agree with each other in supporting the same readings, but they will differ from manuscripts of other families in the readings they support. The following illustrations will help clarify the nature of family agreements.

In Luke's account of the well-known prayer that Jesus taught His disciples (Luke 11:2-4) a number of variations occur. Members of the Western, Caesarean, and Byzantine families agree on 'Our Father who is in heaven', and members of the Alexandrian family agree on 'Father' as the correct reading. Members of the Alexandrian, Caesarean, and Byzantine families agree on 'Let your kingdom come on us'. Members of the Western family agree in reading 'debts' in verse 4 where the other families read 'sins'. Members of the Alexandrian family end the prayer with 'temptation', while members of the other families add 'but deliver us from the evil one' as the conclusion of the prayer.

Putting these data in chart form and assuming in each case that one of the readings is correct and the other incorrect, the families would group themselves in the following manner:

Correct Reading	Support Correct Reading	Support Incorrect Reading
'Father'	Alex.	West., Caes., Byz.
'Let your kingdom come'	Alex., Caes., Byz.	West.
'sins'	Alex., Caes., Byz.	West.
'Do not bear us into temptation'	Alex.	West., Caes., Byz.

In the above hypothesis, members of the Alexandrian family agree with each other in supporting the correct reading all four times, and members of the Western family agree in their support of the incorrect reading all four times. But members of the Caesarean and Byzantine families agree with each other in support of the correct reading twice and in support of the incorrect reading twice. 'Family characteristics' are evident for the Alexandrian and Western families from these four passages. The families distinguish themselves from each other in all four and from the Caesarean and Byzantine in two of the four. From the four illustrations chosen it is impossible, however, to distinguish the Caesarean from the Byzantine because they agree in all four. If one were to add variant readings in other passages, distinctive 'family characteristics' of these two would emerge also.

Multiplied comparisons such as the above have identified four text-types: the Alexandrian, the Western, the Caesarean and the Byzantine. Of these the Byzantine shows the highest correlation to other members of its own family, and the Caesarean the least. Because of the low degree of homogeneity among the Caesarean family members, some have questioned the propriety of calling it a family. But probably enough likenesses exist among family members of this group of documents to justify its being a family too.

Origin of the Families

An important question naturally accompanies an acknowledgment of these families: how did they arise? Apparently early Christian scribes copied the New Testament books according to varying guidelines in different localities of the Mediterranean world. How the families arose we cannot know with certainty. Unfortunately, the ultimate answer to this question is not available in modern times. Nevertheless, answers to two other questions partially satisfy our curiosity in a limited way. The questions are, when and where did these families arise? That information is available with a fairly high degree of certainty through ancient translations and scriptural quotations of early Christian writers.

Earliest ancient translations of the New Testament are in three languages: Syriac, Latin and Coptic. The Syriac language prevailed in the territory of Syria during New Testament times and for several centuries thereafter. Substantial portions of the New Testament in the Syriac language appeared no later than the middle of the second century A.D. The Syriac translation from this period on the whole follows the Western text-type, but it occasionally has readings of the Caesarean type.

Many spoke Latin during these early times in the western Mediterranean regions, including North Africa and Italy. The earliest Latin translation came into existence around A.D. 150, and clearly followed Greek manuscripts of the Western family.

The earliest Coptic translation came about A.D. 200 in the land of Egypt. Manuscripts of this kind fall predominantly in line with the Alexandrian family of readings.

So the ancient versions reflect three text-types that had arisen by the end of the second century A.D. A survey of early church writers who quoted Scripture confirms these times and places for the three families. Tertullian, a second-century North African leader, Irenaeus, a second-century leader in Asia Minor, Italy, and Gaul, and Tatian, a Syrian church leader of the second century, are typical of a large body of writers from these areas who followed the Western-type readings. Clement of Alexandria, another second-century father, usually quotes readings of the Alexandrian type in his writings. Origen, a writer who belongs to the early third century and who spent his later years in Caesarea, chose readings that belonged to the Caesarean family after he moved to Caesarea.

Support for concluding that the Caesarean, the Western, and the Alexandrian families arose in distinct localities by the end of the second century is, therefore, quite solid.

But where was the Byzantine family all this time? The absence of distinctive signs of this family during the beginning centuries of the Christian era is conspicuous. The earliest versional evidence of it is a Syriac translation of the fourth or fifth century, called the Peshitta. The earliest writer whose quotations of Scripture reflect this family of readings is Chrysostom who lived during the late fourth and early fifth centuries. The late appearance of the Byzantine text-type has led most to conclude that it did not exist as a distinct family before the fourth century and that it came together as the result of an effort to bring the other families into alignment with each other. It is a longer text, and its length, at least in part, results from an effort to include as many readings as possible from the other families.

Not everyone accepts the lateness of the Byzantine family's emergence. A few have argued strongly for assigning it a second-century or earlier origin like the other three families. One of the more scholarly of these efforts is that of Sturz who lists one hundred and fifty 'distinctly Byzantine' readings found in second and third century papyri. Yet his list includes readings that could have arisen accidentally, because among his 'distinctively Byzantine' readings are many changes of the type that copyists could have made independently of each other, i.e., without the influence of a 'family' relationship. Nevertheless, the work of Sturz and others has served to awaken the realization that the three families which emerge from the second century do not exhaust all the possible second-century readings. That a few readings were in circulation at that early time which had not found their way into one of the major families is a matter of general acceptance.

How the Byzantine text arose is as much a mystery as how the other families arose. Probably it was a gradual process of revision in which many participated, but at some point an authoritative figure or church body probably issued an edition which culminated the process. At the present all we can do is recognize that it exists as a distinct family that arose later than the others.

Utilizing the Families in Translation
In quest of the genuine (i.e., inspired) text of the New Testament, scholars have differed as to which is the best family. All agree that no family is perfect, but most accept the Alexandrian family as the most reliable of the four. A few view the Western to be superior. An even smaller number endorses the Byzantine as retaining the correct reading most often.

Available English translations represent each of these three families (no English translation uses the Caesarean). The King James Version (also call the Authorized Version) is an example of a New Testament which shows closest kinship to the Byzantine family (*Textus Receptus*, i.e., 'received text', is another title that in general designates this same family). The Douai Version is an example of a version which shows greatest affinity for the Western family. Examples of English translations made from the Alexandrian family are the English Revised Version (1881, 1885) and the American Standard Version (1901).

A pertinent question about the Byzantine family is, how did it come to dominate English translations of the New Testament for so long if it is a secondary or later-in-origin text-type? The answer lies in its dominance of Greek manuscripts of the New Testament from the fifth or sixth century onward. This dominance is explainable perhaps by the relocation of the capital of the Roman Empire from Rome to Asia Minor in the fourth century, and perhaps by growing disuse of the Greek languages in areas outside the Byzantine area (Turkey and Greece in modern times) in these early centuries of the Christian era. In other words, the only Greek manuscripts being produced were in the territory where the Byzantine family was influential.

The dominance of the Byzantine Greek manuscripts through the Middle Ages led to the dominance of the Byzantine family in English translations for so long. When Erasmus edited the first printed Greek New Testament in the early sixteenth century, the only manuscripts available to him were late ones of a Byzantine type. Tyndale depended on this Greek New Testament when he translated his New Testament, the first to be translated from Greek to English. Hence, it was inevitable that Tyndale's work carried this family resemblance.

From then on, practically all new English translations were simply revisions of works done earlier. The Tyndale tradition of dependence on the Byzantine text-type continued through the King James Version of 1611. The King James Version continued its exclusive reign in the English-speaking Protestant church for approximately three and a half centuries.

In the late nineteenth century, however, revisers of the King James Version launched a serious challenge to that textual basis. The challenge came at a time when manuscripts of a more ancient vintage than those available to Erasmus had surfaced. An awareness dawned that the Byzantine family was not the most accurate source for the New Testament text.

The influence of two British scholars, Brook Foss Westcott and Fenton John Anthony Hort, caused that change in appraisal of text-types. The English Revised Version, New Testament, of 1881 translated primarily a Greek text prepared by these two scholars. Their Greek Testament used Alexandrian-type readings rather than Byzantine. Their case for the superior reliability of this family was convincing, so much so that from the turn of the century to the present, most English translations made have been from predominantly Alexandrian sources.

Despite the twentieth-century trend toward the Alexandrian-type translations, some still prefer a Byzantine-based translation. They do so for a variety of reasons. One is the theoretical presumption that the numerical dominance of Greek manuscripts indicates that the Byzantine family is the oldest and therefore the best representative of the original Greek New Testament. This theory, an impressive one on the surface, falters, however, when taking into account the impact of international political and linguistic changes in the early centuries of the Christian era.

Another reason advanced to support the *Textus Receptus* is God's providential care. His providence provided for the preservation of this family in English in the form of the King James Version. The other families were not translated into

English early because they were not inspired, says this theory. This line of reasoning is one-sided. It fails to notice that God's providence provided for the preservation of the Alexandrian and Western families too, text-types preserved in languages other than English. People in other parts of the world have preserved and used those two continuously since the second century. We must accept that God in His providence has seen fit to preserve several families of readings, not just one.

To explain the absence of second-century evidence for the existence of the Byzantine, the pro-Byzantine viewpoint sometimes theorizes that Greek manuscripts of this family were worn out through repeated use because of a recognition of their inspiration, whereas early manuscripts of the other families survived because they experienced only limited use. This explanation is at best highly speculative. Furthermore, it does not explain why the ancient versions and early church writers have no Byzantine readings.

Differences Between the Alexandrian and Byzantine Families
The question often arises: how much difference is there between translations based on different families of manuscripts, particularly the Byzantine and the Alexandrian? Table I provides a partial answer to the question. It lists 165 passages where variations between the two families are noticeable to English readers. The list is by no means an exhaustive list of differences, but presents typical passages where manuscript sources have differing readings of the same passages.

Table I usually does not cite complete verses, only the portions of verses that show the contrasting renderings. The translation is not that of one particular version, but is a literal translation to which any translation can be compared. In the Table contemporary English has been chosen in lieu of Elizabethan English except when Deity is addressed in the text. The Table uses American spellings (e.g., Savior) whenever they differ from English spellings (e.g., Saviour). Readings found in the *Textus Receptus* sometimes differ from the Byzantine family; the Table does not include these (e.g., Acts 9:6a; 1 John 5:7b-8a). Also excluded from consideration are variants where the Byzantine or the Alexandrian family is evenly divided in support of one reading or the other. An English version often indicates that a passage is in doubt by use of brackets or other special markings; in such cases the Table of comparisons assumes the translators' preference for the omission.

TABLE I
COMPARISON OF BYZANTINE AND ALEXANDRIAN FAMILIES IN SELECTED PASSAGES

Reference	Byzantine Supported	Alexandrian Supported
Matthew		
1:25	"firstborn son"	"son"
5:44	"bless those who curse you, do good to those who hate you, and pray for those who despitefully use you and persecute you."	"and pray for those who persecute you."
6:13	"But deliver us from evil. For thine is the kingdom and the power and the glory, forever. Amen."	"But deliver us from evil."
6:33	"the kingdom of God and his righteousness."	"his kingdom and righteousness"
8:29	"Jesus, Son of God"	"Son of God"
9:13	"I have not come to call the righteous, but sinners to repentance."	"I have not come to call the righteous, but sinners."

Reference	Byzantine Supported	Alexandrian Supported
12:35	"the good treasure of the heart"	"the good treasure"
12:47	"Then one said to him, Behold your mother and your brothers stand outside, seeking to speak to you."	*(verse not included)*
13:51	"Jesus says to them, Have you understood all these things? They say to him, Yes, Lord."	"Have you understood all these things? They say to him, Yes."
15:8	"This people draws near to me with their mouth, and honors me with their lips."	"This people honors me with their lips."
16:2-3	"When it is evening...the signs of the times."	*(this portion of v. 2 and v. 3 not included)*
16:13	"Whom do men say that I, the Son of Man, am?"	"Whom do men say that the Son of Man is?"
16:20	"that he was Jesus the Christ"	"that he was the Christ"
17:21	"However, this kind does not go out except by prayer and fasting."	*(verse not included)*
18:11	"For the Son of Man has come to save that which was lost."	*(verse not included)*
19:9	"And the one who marries her who has been put away commits adultery."	*(this portion of verse not included)*
19:17	"there is none good except one, God"	"there is one who is good"
20:7	"You also go into the vineyard, and whatever is right you shall receive."	"You also go into the vineyard."
20:16	"So the last shall be first, and the first last; for many are called, but few chosen."	"So the last shall be first, and the first last."

Reference	Byzantine Supported	Alexandrian Supported
20:22	"Are you able to drink the cup that I shall drink, or to be baptized with the baptism that I am baptized with?"	"Are you able to drink the cup that I shall drink?"
23:14	"Woe to you, scribes and Pharisees, hypocrites! For you devour widows' houses and for a pretense make long prayers; therefore you shall receive the greater damnation."	*(verse not included)*
25:13	"Watch, therefore; for you know neither the day nor the hour in which the Son of Man comes."	"Watch, therefore; for you know neither the day nor the hour."
27:35	"And they crucified him, and divided up his garments, casting lots, that it might be fulfilled which was spoken by the prophet, they divided up my garments among themselves, and over my vesture they cast lots."	"And they crucified him, and divided up his garments, casting lots."
28:2	"for the angel of the Lord descended from heaven, and came and rolled back the stone from the door."	"for the angel of the Lord descended from heaven, and came and rolled back the stone."
28:9	"And as they were going to tell his disciples, behold, Jesus met them, saying,"	"And behold, Jesus met them, saying,"
Mark		
1:2	"As it is written in the prophets"	"As it is written in Isaiah the prophet"
1:14	"preaching the gospel of the kingdom of God"	"preaching the gospel of God"
1:31	"and immediately the fever left her"	"and the fever left her"

Reference	Byzantine Supported	Alexandrian Supported
6:11	"Verily I say to you, It shall be more tolerable for Sodom and Gomorrah in the day of judgment than for that city."	*(this portion of verse not included)*
6:16	"he has risen from the dead"	"he has risen"
6:33	"got there ahead of them, and came together to him"	"got there ahead of them"
7:8	"you hold the tradition of men, the washing of pots and cups, and many other such like things you do."	"you hold the tradition of men."
7:16	"If any man have ears to hear, let him hear."	*(verse not included)*
9:24	"and said with tears, Lord, I believe"	"and said, I believe"
9:44	"Where their worm does not die, and the fire is not quenched"	*(verse not included)*
9:46	"Where their worm does not die, and the fire is not quenched"	*(verse not included)*
9:49	"For everyone shall be salted with fire, and every sacrifice shall be salted with salt."	"For everyone shall be salted with fire."
10:21	"come, take up the cross, and follow me"	"come, follow me"
10:24	"how hard it is for those who trust in riches to enter into the kingdom of God!"	"how hard it is to enter into the kingdom of God!"
11:10	"Blessed be the kingdom of our father David, that comes in the name of the Lord."	"Blessed is the coming kingdom of our father David."

Reference	*Byzantine Supported*	*Alexandrian Supported*
11:26	"But if you do not forgive, neither will your Father who is in heaven forgive your trespasses."	*(verse not included)*
13:14	"the abomination of desolation, spoken of by Daniel the prophet, standing where it should not be"	"the abomination of desolation, standing where it should not be"
14:68	"And he went out onto the porch; and the cock crew."	"And he went out onto the porch."
15:28	"And the Scripture was fulfilled, which says, And he was numbered with transgressors."	*(verse not included)*
16:9-20	"Now when Jesus had risen early the first day of the week...confirming the word with signs following. Amen."	*(verses 9-20 not included)*

Luke

1:28	"The Lord is with you; blessed are you among women."	"The Lord is with you."
2:14	"and on earth peace, good will toward men."	"and on earth peace among men with whom he is pleased."
2:33	"And Joseph and his mother marveled."	"And his father and mother marveled."
2:43	"and Joseph and his mother did not know of it"	"and his parents did not know of it"
4:4	"Man shall not live by bread alone, but by every word of God."	"Man shall not live by bread alone."
4:8	"said to him, Get behind me, Satan; it is written, You shall worship the Lord your God."	"said to him, It is written, You shall worship the Lord your God."

Reference	Byzantine Supported	Alexandrian Supported
4:41	"Thou art Christ, the Son of God."	"Thou art the Son of God."
6:48	"for it was founded upon a rock"	"for it had been well built"
8:43	"a woman having an issue of blood twelve years, who had spent all her living on physicians"	"a woman having an issue of blood twelve years"
9:54	"do you desire that we command fire to come down from heaven and consume them, even as Elijah did?"	"do you desire that we command fire to come down from heaven and consume them?"
9:55	"he turned and rebuked them, and said, You do not know what kind of spirit you are"	"he turned and rebuked them"
9:56	"For the Son of Man has not come to destroy men's lives, but to save them."	*(this portion of verse not included)*
11:2	"Our Father who is in heaven, Hallowed be thy name, thy kingdom come, Thy will be done, as in heaven, so in earth."	"Father, Hallowed be thy name, thy kingdom come."
11:4	"And lead us not into temptation, but deliver us from evil."	"And lead us not into temptation."
11:29	"but the sign of Jonah the prophet"	"but the sign of Jonah"
21:4	"For all these of their abundance have cast into the offerings of God."	"For all these of their abundance have cast into the offerings."
22:31	"And the Lord said, Simon, Simon."	"Simon, Simon."
22:64	"And when they had blindfolded him, they struck him on the face, and asked him,"	"And when they had blindfolded him, they asked him,"

Reference	Byzantine Supported	Alexandrian Supported
23:17	"(For of necessity he must release one to them at the feast.)"	(verse not included)
23:38	"And a superscription also was written over him in letters of Greek and Latin and Hebrew, This is the King of the Jews."	"And a superscription was over him, This is the King of the Jews."
23:42	"And he said to Jesus, Lord, remember me when thou comest into thy kingdom."	"And he said, Jesus, remember me when thou comest into thy kingdom."
24:49	"tarry in the city of Jerusalem"	"tarry in the city"
24:53	"And were continually in the temple, praising and blessing God."	"And were continually in the temple, praising God."

John

1:27	"It is he who coming after me is preferred before me."	"It is he who comes after me."
3:13	"he who came down from heaven, the Son of Man who is in heaven."	"he who came down from heaven, the Son of Man"
3:15	"that whoever believes in him should not perish, but have eternal life."	"that whoever believes in him may have eternal life."
4:42	"this is indeed the Christ, the Savior of the world"	"this is indeed the Savior of the world"
5:3	"waiting for the moving of the water"	(this portion of verse not included)
5:4	"For an angel went down at a certain season into the pool, and troubled the water; whoever then first after the troubling of the water stepped in was	(verse not included)

Reference	*Byzantine Supported*	*Alexandrian Supported*
	made whole of whatever disease he had."	
6:47	"He who believes in me has eternal life."	"He who believes has eternal life."
6:69	"Thou art the Christ, the Son of the living God."	"Thou art the holy one of God."
7:53-8:11	"And every man went into his own house....go, and sin no more."	*(7:53-8:11 not included)*
8:59	"went out of the temple, going through the midst of them, and so passed by."	"went out of the temple"
9:35	"Do you believe in the Son of God?"	"Do you believe in the Son of Man?"
11:41	"Then they took away the stone from the place where the dead was laid."	"Then they took away the stone."
16:16	"and again, a little while, and you shall see me, because I go to the Father."	"and again, a little while, and you shall see me."
17:12	"While I was with them in the world."	"While I was with them"
Acts		
2:30	"God had sworn with an oath to him, that of the fruit of his loins, according to the flesh, he would raise up Christ to sit on his throne."	"God had sworn with an oath to him that he would seat one of the fruit of his loins on his throne."
7:30	"an angel of the Lord"	"an angel"
15:17-18	"says the Lord, who does all things. Known to God are all his works from of old."	"says the Lord, who makes these things known from of old."
16:31	"Believe in the Lord Jesus Christ."	"Believe in the Lord Jesus."

Reference	Byzantine Supported	Alexandrian Supported
17:26	"He made of one blood every nation of men"	"He made of one every nation of men"
20:25	"preaching the kingdom of God"	"preaching the kingdom"
20:32	"And now, brethren, I commend you to God."	"And now I commend you to God."
23:9	"We find no evil in this man; but if a spirit or an angel has spoken to him, let us not fight against God."	"We find no evil in this man; perhaps a spirit or an angel has spoken to him."
24:15	"a resurrection of the dead"	"a resurrection"
28:16	"When we came to Rome, the centurion delivered the prisoners to the captain of the guard; but Paul was permitted to stay by himself, with the soldier who guarded him."	"When we came to Rome, Paul was permitted to stay by himself, with the soldier who guarded him."
28:29	"And when he had said these things, the Jews departed and had a great dispute among themselves."	*(verse not included)*

Romans

1:16	"I am not ashamed of the gospel of Christ"	"I am not ashamed of the gospel."
1:29	"being filled with all unrighteousness, fornication, wickedness, covetousness"	"being filled with all unrighteousness, wickedness, covetousness"
8:1	"There is therefore now no condemnation to those who are in Christ Jesus, who walk not after the flesh, but after the Spirit."	"There is therefore now no condemnation to those who are in Christ Jesus."
9:28	"For he will finish the work, and cut it short in righteousness, because a short work will the Lord make upon the earth."	"For the Lord will do his work upon the earth, finishing it and cutting it short."

Reference	Byzantine Supported	Alexandrian Supported
10:15	"How beautiful are the feet of those who preach the gospel of peace and bring good tidings of good things."	"How beautiful are the feet of those who bring good tidings of good things."
10:17	"the word of God"	"the word of Christ"
11:6	"But if it is of works, then it is no longer of grace; otherwise work is no longer work."	*(this portion of verse not included)*
14:6	"He who observes the day, observes it for the Lord, and who does not observe the day, does not observe it for the Lord."	"He who observes the day, observes it for the Lord."
14:10	"the judgment seat of Christ"	"the judgment seat of God"
15:29	"I shall come in the fullness of the blessing of the gospel of Christ."	"I shall come in the fullness of the blessing of Christ."
16:24	"The grace of our Lord Jesus Christ be with you all. Amen."	*(verse not included)*

1 Corinthians

5:7	"Christ our passover has been sacrificed for us."	"Christ our passover has been sacrificed."
6:20	"therefore glorify God in your body and in your spirit, which are God's."	"therefore glorify God in your body."
7:5	"that you may give yourselves to fasting and prayer"	"that you may give yourselves to prayer"
7:39	"the wife is bound by the law as long as her husband lives"	"the wife is bound as long as her husband lives"
10:28	"for the earth is the Lord's, and the fullness thereof"	*(this portion of verse not included)*
11:24	"Take, eat; this is my body, which is broken for you; this do in remembrance of me."	"This is my body, which is for you; this do in remembrance of me."

Reference	Byzantine Supported	Alexandrian Supported
11:29	"not discerning the Lord's body"	"not discerning the body"
15:47	"the second man is the Lord from heaven"	"the second man is from heaven"
16:22	"If anyone does not love the Lord Jesus Christ"	"if anyone does not love the Lord"
16:23	"The grace of our Lord Jesus Christ be with you."	"The grace of the Lord Jesus be with you."

2 Corinthians

11:31	"The God and Father of our Lord Jesus Christ"	"The God and Father of the Lord Jesus"

Galatians

3:1	"O foolish Galatians, who has bewitched you that you should not obey the truth?"	"O foolish Galatians, who has bewitched you?"
3:17	"the covenant that was confirmed before by God in Christ"	"the covenant that was confirmed before by God"
4:7	"and if a son, then an heir of God through Christ"	"and if a son, then an heir through God"

Ephesians

3:9	"God, who created all things by Jesus Christ"	"God, who created all things"
3:14	"For this cause I bow my knees to the Father of our Lord Jesus Christ."	"For this cause I bow my knees to the Father."
5:30	"For we are members of his body, of his flesh and of his bones."	"For we are members of his body."
6:10	"Finally, my brethren, be strong in the Lord."	"Finally, be strong in the Lord."

Reference	Byzantine Supported	Alexandrian Supported

Philippians

| 3:16 | "let us walk by the same rule, let us mind the same thing" | "let us walk by the same" |

Colossians

| 1:28 | "perfect in Christ Jesus" | "perfect in Christ" |
| 2:11 | "in putting off the body of the sins of the flesh" | "in putting off the body of the flesh" |

1 Thessalonians

| 3:11 | "our Lord Jesus Christ" | "our Lord Jesus" |

1 Timothy

1:17	"the only wise God"	"the only God"
2:7	"I speak the truth in Christ"	"I speak the truth"
3:16	"God was manifest in the flesh"	"who was manifest in the flesh"
4:12	"in word, in behavior, in love, in spirit, in faith, in purity."	"in word, in behavior, in love, in faith, in purity."
5:21	"I charge you before God and the Lord Jesus Christ"	"I charge you before God and Christ Jesus"
6:5	"from such withdraw yourself"	*(this portion of verse not included)*

2 Timothy

| 1:11 | "a preacher and an apostle and a teacher of the Gentiles" | "a preacher and an apostle and a teacher" |
| 4:22 | "The Lord Jesus Christ be with your spirit." | "The Lord be with your spirit." |

Titus

| 1:4 | "from God the Father and the Lord Jesus Christ our Savior" | "from God the Father and Christ Jesus our Savior" |

Reference	*Byzantine Supported*	*Alexandrian Supported*

Philemon

6   "every good thing which is in you in Christ Jesus"   "every good thing which is in you in Christ"

12   "whom I have sent again; now you receive him, that is, my own heart"   "whom I have sent to you, himself, that is, my own heart"

Hebrews

1:3   "when he had by himself purged our sins"   "when he had purged sins"

7:21   "Thou art a priest forever after the order of Melchizedek"   "Thou art a priest forever"

10:30   "Vengeance is mine, I will recompense, says the Lord."   "Vengeance is mine, I will recompense."

10:34   "you have in heaven a better and an enduring substance"   "you have a better and an enduring substance"

11:11   "Through faith also Sarah herself received strength to conceive seed, and was delivered of a child when she was past age."   "Through faith also Sarah herself received strength to conceive seed, even beyond the proper time of life"

James

5:16   "Confess your faults to one another."   "Confess your sins to one another."

1 Peter

1:22   "you have purified your souls in obeying the truth through the Spirit to unfeigned love of the brethren"   "you have purified your souls in obeying the truth to unfeigned love of the brethren"

3:15   "sanctify the Lord God in your hearts"   "sanctify Christ as Lord in your hearts"

4:1   "Christ has suffered for us in the flesh"   "Christ has suffered in the flesh"

Reference	Byzantine Supported	Alexandrian Supported
4:14	"on their part he is evil spoken of, but on your part he is glorified"	*(this portion of verse not included)*

2 Peter

2:17	"for whom the mist of darkness is reserved forever"	"for whom the mist of darkness is reserved"
3:9	"longsuffering toward us"	"longsuffering toward you"

1 John

1:7	"the blood of Jesus Christ his Son"	"the blood of Jesus his Son"
2:7	"the word which you have heard from the beginning"	"the word which you have heard"
3:1	"that we should be called the children of God"	"that we should be called the children of God, and we are"
4:3	"every spirit that does not confess that Jesus Christ has come in the flesh"	"every spirit that does not confess Jesus"
4:19	"We love him, because he first loved us."	"We love, because he first loved us."
5:13	"and that you may believe on the name of the Son of God."	*(this portion of verse not included)*

Jude

25	"to the only wise God"	"to the only God"

Revelation

1:8	"I am Alpha and Omega, the beginning and the ending."	"I am Alpha and Omega."
1:9	"patience of Jesus Christ"	"patience in Jesus"
1:11	"saying, I am Alpha and Omega, the first and the last; and What you see, write in a book."	"saying, What you see, write in a book."

Reference	Byzantine Supported	Alexandrian Supported
2:13	"I know your works and where you dwell"	"I know where you dwell"
*6:1,3 5,7	"Come and see."	"Come."
*8:13	"heard an angel flying"	"heard an eagle flying"
11:17	"who is and who was and who is to come"	"who is and who was"
*16:17	"a great voice out of the temple of heaven"	"a great voice out of the temple"
20:9	"fire came down from God out of heaven"	"fire came down out of heaven"

*The Byzantine family in Revelation is known to have two "strands" or "branches." In these passages this family is represented only by one or the other of these two.

An interesting facet of the passages found in Table I is the manner in which the Byzantine reading differs from the Alexandrian. The difference in almost half the passages is traceable to the attempt of a later copyist to harmonize the passage with some other part of the Bible. For example, the words of Matthew 5:44 that appear in the Byzantine-supported translations but not in the Alexandrian-supported ones, apparently derive from Luke 6:27-28. It is a well-known tendency among the writers of the early part of the Christian era to alter Scripture to bring it into greater agreement with other portions. A noteworthy example of this was Tatian's *Diatessaron* in which he combined the texts of the four Gospels into one continuous narrative of the life of Christ. Quite evidently a good bit of alteration to the individual Gospels was necessary to accomplish this. That characteristic of the Byzantine-type readings is another evidence of their late origin in comparison with the other families.

Family Characteristics of English Translations

Comparing English translations to the 165 passages listed in Table I is very instructive. One can see at a glance the family that served as a basis for a translation of each one of these passages. Though the wording will not coincide exactly with that of Table I, it will approximate one rendering or the other closely enough to reflect which text-type was followed by a translation in that passage.

Table II reflects the results of a comparison carried out with twenty well-known English translations. These include the King James Version (KJV), the New King James Version (NKJV), The Living Bible (LB), The Message (MES), New Living Translation (NLT), New Century Version (NCV), Phillips Modern English (PME), Contemporary English Version (CEV), New English Bible (NEB), New American Bible (NAB), Today's English Version (TEV, also known as the Good News Bible), New Jerusalem Bible (NJB), Jerusalem Bible (JB), Revised English Bible (REB), New Revised Standard Version (NRSV), New International Version (NIV), New American Standard Bible Updated (NASBU), New English Translation (NET), New American Standard Bible (NASB), and Revised Standard Version (RSV). Beneath each version in the Table an 'X' in the left column headed by 'B' indicates agreement with the Byzantine family and an 'X' in the right column headed by 'A' indicates agreement with the Alexandrian family. Occasionally a question mark (?) appears in both columns because the freeness of the translation makes it impossible to tell which reading a version is rendering.

TABLE II

COMPARISON OF SEVERAL TRANSLATIONS TO

BYZANTINE AND ALEXANDRIAN FAMILIES

	KJV		NKJV		LB		MES		NLT		NCV		PME		CEV		NEB		NAB		TEV		NJB		JB		REB		NRSV		NIV		NASBU		NET		NASB		RSV	
	B	A	B	A	B	A	B	A	B	A	B	A	B	A	B	A	B	A	B	A	B	A	B	A	B	A	B	A	B	A	B	A	B	A	B	A	B	A	B	A
MATT. 1:25	X		X			X		X		X		X		X		X		X		X		X		X		X		X		X		X		X		X		X		X
5:44	X		X			X		X		X		X		X		X		X		X		X		X		X		X		X		X		X		X		X		X
6:13	X		X			X		X		X		X		X		X		X		X		X		X		X		X		X		X		X		X		X		X
6:33	X		X			X	X		X		X		X		X		X		X		X		X		X		X		X		X		X		X		X		X
8:29	X		X			X	X			X		X		X	X			X		X		X		X		X		X		X		X		X		X		X		X
9:13	X		X		X			X		X		X		X	X			X		X		X		X		X		X		X		X		X		X		X		X
12:35	X		X			X		X		X		X		X		X		X		X		X		X		X		X		X		X		X		X		X		X
12:47	X		X			X		X		X		X		X		X		X		X		X		X		X		X		X		X	X			X		X		X
13:51	X		X			X		X		X		X		X		X		X		X		X		X		X		X		X		X		X		X		X		X
15:8	X		X			X		X		X		X		X		X		X		X		X		X		X		X		X		X		X		X		X		X
16:2-3	X		X			X		X		X		X		X		X		X		X		X		X		X		X		X		X		X		X		X	X	
16:13	X		X			X		X		X		X		X		X		X		X		X		X		X		X		X		X		X		X		X		X
16:20	X		X			X		X		X		X		X		X		X		X		X		X		X		X		X		X		X		X		X		X
17:21	X		X		X			X		X		X		X		X		X		X		X		X		X		X		X		X		X		X		X		X
18:11	X		X		X			X		X		X		X		X		X		X		X		X		X		X		X		X		X		X		X		X
19:9	X		X			X		X		X		X		X		X		X	X			X		X		X		X		X		X		X		X		X		X
19:17	X		X			X		X		X		X		X	X			X		X		X		X		X		X		X		X		X		X		X		X
20:7	X		X			X		X		X		X		X		X		X		X		X		X		X		X		X		X		X		X		X		X
20:16	X		X			X		X		X		X		X		X		X		X		X		X		X		X		X		X		X		X		X		X
20:22	X		X			X		X		X		X		X		X		X		X		X		X		X		X		X		X		X		X		X		X
23:14	X		X		X			X		X		X		X		X		X		X		X		X		X		X		X		X		X		X		X		X
25:13	X		X			X		X		X		X		X		X		X		X		X		X		X		X		X		X		X		X		X		X
27:35	X		X			X		X		X		X		X		X		X		X		X		X		X		X		X		X		X		X		X		X
28:2	X		X			X		X		X		X		X		X		X		X		X		X		X		X		X		X		X		X		X		X
28:9	X		X			X		X		X		X		X		X		X		X		X		X		X		X		X		X		X		X		X		X
MARK 1:2	X		X			X		X		X		X		X		X		X		X		X		X		X		X		X		X		X		X		X		X
1:14	X		X		X			X		X		X		X		X		X		X		X		X		X		X		X		X		X		X		X		X
1:31	X		X			X		X		X		X		X		X		X		X		X		X		X		X		X		X		X		X		X		X
6:11	X		X			X		X		X		X		X		X		X		X		X		X		X		X		X		X		X		X		X		X
6:16	X		X			X		X		X		X	X			X		X		X		X		X		X		X		X		X		X		X		X		X

	KJV		NKJV		LB		MES		NLT		NCV		PME		CEV		NEB		NAB		TEV		NJB		JB		REB		NRSV		NIV		NASBU		NET		NASB		RSV	
	B	A	B	A	B	A	B	A	B	A	B	A	B	A	B	A	B	A	B	A	B	A	B	A	B	A	B	A	B	A	B	A	B	A	B	A	B	A	B	A
MARK 6:33	X		X		X		X		X		X		X		X		X		X		X		X		X		X		X		X		X		X		X		X
7:8	X		X		X		X		X		X		X		X		X		X		X		X		X		X		X		X		X		X		X		X
7:16	X		X		X		X		X		X		X		X		X		X		X		X		X		X		X		X		X		X		X		X
9:24	X		X		X		X		X		X		X		X		X		X		X		X		X		X		X		X		X		X		X		X
9:44	X		X		X		X		X		X		X		X		X		X		X		X		X		X		X		X		X		X		X		X
9:46	X		X		X		X		X		X		X		X		X		X		X		X		X		X		X		X		X		X		X		X
9:49	X		X		X		X		X		X		X		X		X		X		X		X		X		X		X		X		X		X		X		X
10:21	X		X		X		X		X		X		X		X		X		X		X		X		X		X		X		X		X		X		X		X
10:24	X		X			X		X		X		X		X		X		X		X		X		X		X		X		X		X		X		X		X		X
11:10	X		X		X		X		X		X		X		X		X		X		X		X		X		X		X		X		X		X		X		X
11:26	X		X		X		X		X		X		X		X		X		X		X		X		X		X		X		X		X		X		X		X
13:14	X		X		X		X		X		X		X		X		X		X		X		X		X		X		X		X		X		X		X		X
14:68	X		X			X		X		X		X		X		X		X		X		X		X		X		X		X		X		X		X		X		X
15:28	X		X		X		X		X		X		X		X		X		X		X		X		X		X		X		X		X		X		X		X
16:9-20	X		X		X		X		X		X		X		X		X		X		X		X		X		X		X		X		X		X		X		X
LUKE 1:28	X		X		X		X		X		X		X		X		X		X		X		X		X		X		X		X		X		X		X		X
2:14	X		X		X		X		X		X		X		X		X		X		X			X	X		X		X		X		X		X		X		X
2:33	X		X		X		X		X		X		X		X		X		X		X		X		X		X		X		X		X		X		X		X
2:43	X		X		X		X		X		X		X		X		X		X		X		X		X		X		X		X		X		X		X		X
4:4	X		X		X		X		X		X		X		X		X		X		X		X		X		X		X		X		X		X		X		X
4:8	X		X		X		X		X		X		X		X		X		X		X		X		X		X		X		X		X		X		X		X
4:41	X		X		X		X		X		X		X		X		X		X		X		X		X		X		X		X		X		X		X		X
6:48	X		X		X		X		X		X		X		X		X		X		X		X		X		X		X		X		X		X		X		X
8:43	X		X		X		X		X		X		X		X		X		X		X		X		X		X		X		X		X		X		X		X
9:54	X		X		X		X		X		X		X		X		X		X		X		X		X		X		X		X		X		X		X		X
9:55	X		X		X		X		X		X		X		X		X		X		X		X		X		X		X		X		X		X		X		X
9:56	X		X		X		X		X		X		X		X		X		X		X		X		X		X		X		X		X		X		X		X
11:2	X		X		X		X		X		X		X		X		X		X		X		X		X		X		X		X		X		X		X		X
11:4	X		X		X		X		X		X		X		X		X		X		X		X		X		X		X		X		X		X		X		X
11:29	X		X		X		X		X		X		X		X		X		X		X		X		X		X		X		X		X		X		X		X
21:4	X		X		X		X		X		X		X		X		X		X		X		X		X		X		X		X		X		X		X		X
22:31	X		X		X		X		X		X		X		X		X		X		X		X		X		X		X		X		X		X		X		X
22:64	X		X		X		X		X		X		X		X		X		X		X		X		X		X		X		X		X		X		X		X
23:17	X		X		X		X		X		X		X		X		X		X		X		X		X		X		X		X		X		X		X		X
23:38	X		X		X		X		X		X		X		X		X		X		X		X		X		X		X		X		X		X		X		X
23:42	X		X		X		X		X		X		X		X		X		X		X		X		X		X		X		X		X		X		X		X
24:49	X		X		X		X		X		X		X		X		X		X		X		X		X		X		X		X		X		X		X		X
24:53	X		X		X		X		X		X		X		X		X		X		X		X		X		X		X		X		X		X		X		X
JOHN 1:27	X		X		X		X		X		X		X		X		X		X		X		X		X		X		X		X		X		X		X		X

	KJV		NKJV		LB		MES		NLT		NCV		PME		CEV		NEB		NAB		TEV		NJB		JB		REB		NRSV		NIV		NASBU		NET		NASB		RSV	
	B	A	B	A	B	A	B	A	B	A	B	A	B	A	B	A	B	A	B	A	B	A	B	A	B	A	B	A	B	A	B	A	B	A	B	A	B	A	B	A
JOHN 3:13	X		X			X	X			X		X		X		X		X		X		X		X		X		X		X		X		X		X		X		X
3:15	X		X			X	X			X		X		X		X	X			X		X		X		X		X		X		X		X		X		X		X
4:42	X		X			X		X		X		X		X		X	X			X		X		X	X			X		X		X		X		X		X		X
5:3	X		X		X			X		X		X	X			X		X		X		X		X	X			X		X		X		X		X	X			X
5:4	X		X		X		X			X		X	X			X		X		X		X		X	X			X		X		X		X		X		X	X	
6:47	X		X		X			X		X		X		X	X			X		X		X		X		X		X		X		X		X		X		X		X
6:69	X		X		X			X	X			X	X		X			X		X		X		X		X		X		X		X		X		X		X		X
7:53-8:11	X		X			X		X		X		X		X		X		X		X		X	X			X		X		X		X		X		X		X		X
8:59	X		X			X	X			X		X		X		X		X		X		X		X		X		X		X		X		X		X		X		X
9:35	X		X			X		X		X		X		X		X		X		X		X		X		X		X		X		X		X		X		X		X
11:41	X		X			X		X		X		X		X		X		X		X		X		X		X		X		X		X		X		X		X		X
16:16	X		X			X		X		X		X		X		X		X		X		X		X		X		X		X		X		X		X		X		X
17:12	X		X			X		X		X		X		X		X		X		X		X		X		X		X		X		X		X		X		X		X
ACTS 2:30	X		X			X	X			X		X		X		X		X		X		X		X		X		X		X		X		X		X		X		X
7:30	X		X			X	X			X		X		X		X		X		X		X		X		X		X		X		X		X		X		X		X
15:17-18	X		X			X		X		X		X		X		X		X		X		X		X		X	X			X		X		X		X		X		X
16:31	X		X			X		X		X		X		X		X		X	X			X		X		X	X			X		X		X		X		X		X
17:26	X		X			X	X			X		X	X			X		X		X	X			X		X		X		X		X		X		X		X		X
20:25	X		X			X	X			X		X		X		X		X		X	X			X		X		X		X		X		X		X		X		X
20:32	X		X			X	X			X		X		X		X		X		X		X		X		X		X		X		X		X		X		X		X
23:9	X		X			X	X			X		X		X	X			X		X		X		X		X		X		X		X		X		X		X		X
24:15	X		X			X		X		X		X		X		X		X		X		X		X		X		X		X		X		X		X		X		X
28:16	X		X			X		X		X		X		X		X		X		X		X		X		X		X		X		X		X		X		X		X
28:29	X		X			X		X		X		X		X		X		X		X		X		X		X		X		X		X		X		X		X		X
ROMANS 1:16	X		X		X			X		X		X		X		X		X		X		X		X		X		X		X		X		X		X		X		X
1:29	X		X			X		X		X		X		X		X		X		X		X		X		X		X		X		X		X		X		X		X
8:1	X		X			X		X	X			X		X		X		X		X		X		X		X		X		X		X		X		X		X		X
9:28	X		X		X			X		X		X		X		X		X		X		X		X		X		X		X		X		X		X		X		X
10:15	X		X			X		X		X		X		X		X		X		X		X		X		X		X		X		X		X		X		X		X
10:17	X		X			X		X		X		X		X		X		X		X		X		X		X		X		X		X		X		X		X		X
11:6	X		X			X		X	X			X		X		X		X		X		X		X		X		X		X		X		X		X		X		X
14:6	X		X			X		X		X		X		X		X		X		X		X		X		X		X		X		X		X		X		X		X
14:10	X		X			X	X			X		X		X		X		X		X		X		X		X		X		X		X		X		X		X		X
15:29	X		X			X		X		X		X		X		X		X		X		X		X		X		X		X		X		X		X		X		X
16:24	X		X			X		X		X		X	X			X		X		X		X		X		X		X		X		X		X		X		X		X
1 COR. 5:7	X		X		X		X		X			X		X		X		X		X		X		X		X		X		X		X		X		X		X		X
6:20	X		X			X	X			X		X		X		X		X		X		X		X		X		X		X		X		X		X		X		X
7:5	X		X			X	X			X		X		X		X		X		X		X		X		X		X		X		X		X		X		X		X
7:39	X		X			X	X			X		X		X		X		X		X		X		X		X		X		X		X		X		X		X		X

	KJV		NKJV		LB		MES		NLT		NCV		PME		CEV		NEB		NAB		TEV		NJB		JB		REB		NRSV		NIV		NASBU		NET		NASB		RSV	
	B	A	B	A	B	A	B	A	B	A	B	A	B	A	B	A	B	A	B	A	B	A	B	A	B	A	B	A	B	A	B	A	B	A	B	A	B	A	B	A
1COR. 10:28	X		X		X		X		X		X		X		X		X		X		X		X		X		X		X		X		X		X		X		X	
11:24	X		X		X		X		X		X		X		X		X		X		X		X		X		X		X		X		X		X		X		X	
11:29	X		X			X	X		X		X		X		X		X		X		X		X		X		X		X		X		X		X		X		X	
15:47	X		X		X		X		X		X		X		X		X		X		X		X		X		X		X		X		X		X		X		X	
16:22	X		X			X	X		X		X		X		X		X		X		X		X		X		X		X		X		X		X		X		X	
16:23	X		X			X	X		X		X		X		X		X		X		X		X		X		X		X		X		X		X		X		X	
2 COR. 11:31	X		X		X		X		X		X		X		X		X		X		X		X		X		X		X		X		X		X		X		X	
GAL. 3:1	X		X		X		X		X			X	X		X		X		X		X		X		X		X		X		X		X		X		X		X	
3:17	X		X		X		X		X		X		X		X		X		X		X		X		X		X		X		X		X		X		X		X	
4:7	X		X		X		X		X		X		X		X		X		X		X		X		X		X		X		X		X		X		X		X	
EPH. 3:9	X		X		X		X		X		X		X		X		X		X		X		X		X		X		X		X		X		X		X		X	
3:14	X		X		X		X		X		X		X		X		X		X		X		X		X		X		X		X		X		X		X		X	
5:10	X		X		X		X		X		X		X		X		X		X		X		X		X		X		X		X		X		X		X		X	
6:10	X		X		X		X		X		X		X		X		X		X		X		X		X		X		X		X		X		X		X		X	
PHIL. 3:16	X		X		X		X		X		X		X		X		X		X		X		X		X		X		X		X		X		X		X		X	
COL. 1:28	X		X		X		X		X		X		X		X		X		X		X		X		X		X		X		X		X		X		X		X	
2:11	X		X		X		X		X		X		X		X		X		X		X		X		X		X		X		X		X		X		X		X	
1 THES. 3:11	X		X		X		X		X		X		X		X		X		X		X		X		X		X		X		X		X		X		X		X	
1 TIM. 1:17	X		X		X		X		X		X		X		X		X		X		X		X		X		X		X		X		X		X		X		X	
2:7	X		X		X		X		X		X		X		X		X		X		X		X		X		X		X		X		X		X		X		X	
3:16	X		X		X		X		X		X		X		X		X		X		X		X		X		X		X		X		X		X		X		X	
4:12	X		X		X		X		X		X		X		X		X		X		X		X		X		X		X		X		X		X		X		X	
5:21	X		X		X		X		X		X		X		X		X		X		X		X		X		X		X		X		X		X		X		X	
6:5	X		X		X		X		X		X		X		X		X		X		X		X		X		X		X		X		X		X		X		X	
2 TIM. 1:11	X		X		X		X		X		X		X		X		X		X		X		X		X		X		X		X		X		X		X		X	
4:22	X		X		X		X		X		X		X		X		X		X		X		X		X		X		X		X		X		X		X		X	
TITUS 1:4	X		X		X		X		X		X		X		X		X		X		X		X		X		X		X		X		X		X		X		X	
PHILEMON 6	X		X		X		X		X		X			X	X		X			X	X		X		X		X		X		X		X		X		X		X	
12	X		X		X		X		X		X		X		X		X		X		X		X		X		X		X		X		X		X		X		X	
HEB. 1:3	X		X		X		X		X		X		X		X		X		X		X		X		X		X		X		X		X		X		X		X	
7:21	X		X		X		X		X		X		X		X		X		X		X		X		X		X		X		X		X		X		X		X	
10:30	X		X		X		X		X		X		X		X		X		X		X		X		X		X		X		X		X		X		X		X	
10:34	X		X		X		X		X		X		X		X		X		X		X		X		X		X		X		X		X		X		X		X	
11:11	X		X		X		X			X	X		X		X		X		X		X		X		X		X		X		X		X		X		X		X	
JAMES 5:16	X		X		X		X		X		X		X		X		X		X		X		X		X		X		X		X		X		X		X		X	
1 PETER 1:22	X		X		X		X		X		X		X		X		X		X		X		X		X		X		X		X		X		X		X		X	
3:15	X		X		X		X		X		X		X		X		X		X		X		X		X		X		X		X		X		X		X		X	
4:1	X		X		X		X		X		X		X		X		X		X		X		X		X		X		X		X		X		X		X		X	
4:14	X		X		X		X		X		X		X		X		X		X		X		X		X		X		X		X		X		X		X		X	

	KJV		NKJV		LB		MES		NLT		NCV		PME		CEV		NEB		NAB		TEV		NJB		JB		REB		NRSV		NIV		NASBU		NET		NASB		RSV	
	B	A	B	A	B	A	B	A	B	A	B	A	B	A	B	A	B	A	B	A	B	A	B	A	B	A	B	A	B	A	B	A	B	A	B	A	B	A	B	A
2 PETER 2:17	X		X		X		X		X		X		X		X		X		X		X		X		X		X		X		X		X		X		X		X
3:9	X		X		?		X		X		X		X		X		X		X		X		X		X		X		X		X		X		X		X		X
1 JOHN 1:7	X		X		X		X		X		X		X		X		X		X		X		X		X		X		X		X		X		X		X		X
2:7	X		X		X		X		X		X		X		X		X		X		X		X		X		X		X		X		X		X		X		X
3:1	X		X		?		X			X	X		X		X		X		X		X		X		X		X		X		X		X		X		X		X
4:3	X		X				X		X		X		X		X		X		X		X		X		X		X		X		X		X		X		X		X
4:19	X		X		X		X		X		X		X		X		X		X		X		X		X		X		X		X		X		X		X		X
5:13	X		X		?		X		X		X		X		X		X		X		X		X		X		X		X		X		X		X		X		X
JUDE 25	X		X		?		X		X		X		X		X		X		X		X		X		X		X		X		X		X		X		X		X
REV. 1:8	X		X		X		X		X		X		X		X		X		X		X		X		X		X		X		X		X		X		X		X
1:9	X		X		X		X		X		X		X		X		X		X		X		X		X		X		X		X		X		X		X		X
1:11	X		X		X		X		X			X	X		X		X		X		X		X		X		X		X		X		X		X		X		X
2:13	X		X		X		X		X		X		X		X		X		X		X		X		X		X		X		X		X		X		X		X
6:1,3,5,7	X		X		X		X		X		X		X		X		X		X		X		X		X		X		X		X		X		X		X		X
8:13	X		X		X		X		X		X		X		X		X		X		X		X		X		X		X		X		X		X		X		X
11:17	X		X		X		X		X		X		X		X		X		X		X		X		X		X		X		X		X		X		X		X
16:17	X		X		X		X		X		X		X		X		X		X		X		X		X		X		X		X		X		X		X		X
20:9	X		X		X		X		X		X		X		X		X		X		X		X		X		X		X		X		X		X		X		X

One may tabulate the results of surveying the 165 selected passages regarding their textual basis in Table II. That tabulation reflects how frequently each translation follows a Byzantine family reading and how frequently an Alexandrian family reading.

Table III reflects this indication of textual basis. It is well to repeat that the list does not exhaust the passages where family variations appear, but the Table is fairly representative of how close a version is to each of these text types. In a few cases the total of the two columns does not come to 165. In those cases question marks (?) indicate that the textual basis of a reading is uncertain.

TABLE III
STATISTICAL SUMMARY OF TABLE II

Version Name	Byzantine Readings	Alexandrian Readings
King James Version	165	0
New King James Version	165	0
Living Bible	43 + 3?	129 + 3?
The Message	22	143
New Living Translation	21 + 1?	143 + 1?
New Century Version	16	149
Phillips Modern English	15	150
Contemporary English Version	13 + 2?	150 + 2?
New English Bible	8 + 1?	156 + 1?
New American Bible	8	157
Today's English Version	7	158
New Jerusalem Bible	7	158
Jerusalem Bible	6	159
Revised English Bible	6	159
New Revised Standard Version	5	160
New International Version	5 + 1?	159 + 1?
New American Standard Bible Updated	3	162
NET Bible	3	162
New American Standard Bible	2	163
Revised Standard Version	1	164

The results of the survey of these versions show that most tend to follow the Alexandrian class of readings. Only two, the King James and the New King James, use the Byzantine. Percentage agreements are not too meaningful because the list of passages is not exhaustive, but it is of interest to rank the translations in the order of their closeness to the Alexandrian family in this set of passages. The resulting order is RSV, NASB, NASBU, NIV, NRSV, REB, JB, NJB, TEV, NAB, NEB, CEV, PME, NCV, NLT, MES, and LB. (The NIrV follows the same textual basis as the NIV). The last in this sequence is the Living Bible, but it still agrees with the Alexandrian reading in 86% of these 165 passages.

Also of note are free translations and paraphrases (see next chapter for a discussion of the translation techniques) whose translations in several instances are so free that it is impossible to tell what Greek text they are rendering. Table II above indicates those instances with a question mark in both the Byzantine (B) and Alexandrian (A) columns.

Anyone who desires may make a comparison of his own for other versions besides those found in Tables II and III by comparing each version with the two possible renderings for each passage in Table I. The rendering will resemble one of the two columns in the Table more closely, telling what family of texts was the basis for that particular passage.

The Preferred Original Text

In summary of this brief survey of original texts that serve as a basis for translations of the Bible, the main task in choosing a text pertains to the New Testament rather than the Old. Issues pertaining to the Old Testament are relatively uninvolved when compared to the variations in New Testament sources which are far more numerous than those for the Old Testament.

For most English Bible users the New Testament

translation chosen boils down to a decision between two families of manuscript readings, the Byzantine and the Alexandrian. Many have opted for and will continue to opt for the Byzantine text-type, largely because of the widespread and long-standing influence of the King James Version. Arguments mustered for this preference will most likely be less significant in the minds of most.

On the other hand, others will join the growing constituency in support of the Alexandrian supported translations. When all is said and done, the stronger evidence in all probability supports this category of readings as being closer to the very words that were written by the original authors of the New Testament books. As our study has shown, this is the choice that has been made in most contemporary-English translations in recent years.

Selected Reading List

Aland, Kurt, and Barbara Aland. *The Text of the New Testament.* Erroll F. Rhodes, trans.; Grand Rapids: Eerdmans, 1987.

Carson, D. A. *The King James Debate.* Grand Rapids: Baker, 1979.

Fee, Gordon D. 'Modern Textual Criticism and the Revival of the Textus Receptus,' *Journal of the Evangelical Theological Society.* 21:1 (March 1978): 19-33.

_____. 'Modern Textual Criticism and the Majority Text: A Rejoinder,' *Journal of the Evangelical Theological Society.* 21:2 (June 1978): 157-160.

Greenlee, J. Harold. *Introduction to New Testament Textual Criticism.* Grand Rapids: Eerdmans, 1964.

Harrison, E. F. *Introduction to the New Testament.* Grand Rapids: Eerdmans, 1971. 63-84.

Harrison, R. K., B. K. Waltke, D. Guthrie, and G. D. Fee. *Biblical Criticism: Historical, Literary, Textual.* Grand Rapids: Zondervan, 1978. 47-84, 127-158.

Hodges, Zane C. 'Modern Textual Criticism and the Majority

Text: A Response,' *Journal of the Evangelical Theological Society*. 21:2 (June 1978): 143-155.

Hodges, Zane C., and Arthur L. Farstad (eds.). *The Greek New Testament According to the Majority Text*. Nashville: Nelson, 1982.

Kubo, Sakae, and Walter F. Specht. *So Many Versions?*. Revised Edition. Grand Rapids: Zondervan, 1983.

Metzger, Bruce M. *The Text of the New Testament*. 3rd ed.; New York: Oxford, 1992.

Pickering, Wilbur N. *The Identity of the New Testament Text*. Nashville: Nelson, 1977.

Robertson, A. T. *An Introduction to the Textual Criticism of the New Testament*. Nashville: Broadman, 1925.

Sturz, Harry A. *The Byzantine Text-Type & New Testament Textual Criticism*. Nashville: Nelson, 1984.

Thiessen, Henry Clarence. *An Introduction to the New Testament*. Grand Rapids: Eerdmans, 1943. 31-77.

White, James R. *The King James Only Controversy: Can You Trust Modern Translations?* Minneapolis: Bethany House, 1995.

Chapter 3

TECHNIQUES USED IN
BIBLE TRANSLATIONS

In evaluating English translations of the Bible, a person must make a choice relative to the techniques followed in producing the translations. 'Technique' means the methodology of the translator(s), sometimes referred to as the philosophy of translation. Translators follow different methodologies in view of the varying purposes of their translations. In other words, they have different goals to fulfil or different concepts of what constitutes the process of translation.

Two Philosophies of Translation
Philosophies of translation fall into two general categories. One type is a dynamic-equivalence (or functional-equivalence) translation, and the other a formal-equivalence (or formal-correspondence) translation. Dynamic equivalence results in what is termed more popularly a 'free translation' or a 'paraphrase', while 'literal translations' result from formal-equivalence techniques.

The chief concern of the dynamic-equivalence approach is readability. This philosophy centers on conveying the thought of the original languages to the reader with the greatest possible clarity and gives little or no attention to obtaining a word-for-word correspondence between the original and the translation. It focuses rather on obtaining a correspondence of ideas between the two languages. The important consideration here is to produce an effect on the reader in the receptor language equivalent to what was produced on the original recipients of the message in the source language. If a free translation evokes the same response from its readers as the original did on the readers when the book was first circulated, it has accomplished its purpose. Most late-twentieth-century Bible translations are of this type.

A formal-equivalence translation concerns itself primarily with accuracy or faithfulness to the original text. In both form and content it focuses attention on the original text being translated. It seeks as close a match as possible between the elements of the receptor language and those of the source language. Its reader can thus identify himself as fully as possible with someone in the source-language context and more fully comprehend the customs, manner of thought, and means of expression connected with the original setting. To accomplish this goal, the literal translation preserves as much of the source-language grammatical structures and word usages as the boundaries of proper English will allow. Bible translations in the Tyndale tradition are of this type, but they are not the only literal translations.

Testing the Two Techniques

Linguistic specialists have developed tests to gauge how well translations of both types have achieved their purposes. The 'Cloze Technique' tests how well translations have succeeded in attaining a high degree of readability. It selects a portion of suitable length, perhaps a paragraph, from the translation being tested, and reproduces it with every third or fifth word being replaced with a blank to be filled in. A sampling of people then try to fill in the missing words. How well those persons can fill in correctly the omitted words determines the readability of the passage. If a large number of people tested identify successfully a good proportion of the missing words, the degree of readability is high. That reflects the communicative effectiveness of the translation because it shows people's familiarity with the vocabulary, idiom, and style of the English used in the translation.

That type of test is not always completely satisfactory, because different groups of people differ so widely in their English preferences. A translation that scores well with one group may do very poorly with another group. Readability preferences vary widely in different geographical locations, among different socio-educational groups, because of age differences, and during different periods of history.

The other kind of test is more objective and therefore more satisfactory. That is the test that reflects how close a translation remains to the original text being translated. This is appropriately called the 'deviation' test, since it measures the amount a translation deviates from the original text it translates. William L. Wonderly (cf. Eugene A. Nida, *Toward a Science of Translating* [Leiden: E.J. Brill, 1964], 184-192) developed the test in conjunction with his work for the United Bible Societies. The form of the test outlined below is essentially as Wonderly proposed it, but a few elements differ from his proposal.

Calculating the deviation value for a given passage follows a five-step procedure.

(1) A passage of from thirty to fifty words in the Hebrew or Aramaic Old Testament or the Greek New Testament is selected and its words are numbered consecutively. For purposes of the test, a transliteration of the original text is sufficient.

To illustrate this first step, Matthew 7:19-21 is selected:
^{1}pan ^{2}dendron ^{3}mē ^{4}poioun ^{5}karpon ^{6}kalon ^{7}ekkoptetai ^{8}kai ^{9}eis ^{10}pur ^{11}balletai. ^{12}Ara ^{13}ge ^{14}apo ^{15}tōn ^{16}karpōn ^{17}autōn ^{18}epignōsesthe ^{19}autous. ^{20}Ou ^{21}pas ^{22}ho ^{23}legōn ^{24}moi ^{25}kurie ^{26}kurie, ^{27}eiseleusetai

[28]*eis* [29]*tēn* [30]*basileian* [31]*tōn* [32]*ouranōn,* [34]*all'* [34]*ho* [35]*poiōn* [36]*to* [37]*thelēma* [38]*tou* [39]*patros* [40]*mou* [41]*tou* [42]*en* [43]*tois* [44]*ouranois.*

(2) Next comes a translation of each word into its nearest English equivalent or a literal transfer. That transpires without rearranging the word order. The English equivalents in step two retain the consecutive numbers from step one. This stage retains alternative English renderings for various words. It will result in incomprehensible English for the most part, but it is a necessary intermediate stage.

The 'literal transfer' for Matthew 7:19-21 is as follows: [1]every [2]tree [3]not [4]making [5]fruit [6]good [7]is-cut-down [8]and [9]into [10]fire [11]is-cast. [12]So/therefore [13]indeed [14]from [15]the [16]fruits [17]of-them [18]shall-know [19]them. [20]Not [21]every [22]the [23]one-saying [24]to-me [25]Lord [26]Lord, [27]shall-enter [28]into [29]the [30]kingdom [31]of-the [32]heavens, [33]but [34]the [35]one-doing [36]the [37]will [38]of-the [39]Father [40]of-me [41]the-one [42]in [43]the [44]heavens.

(3) Next in sequence is an adjustment of the English word order and any other changes necessary to bring the section into a readable English format. 'Minimal transfer' is an accurate label for this step. In the process of rearranging words, each word or phrase retains its original sequential number. The step results in the closest accurate and meaningful English equivalent of the Hebrew or Greek text. The closest equivalent translation furnishes a norm with which to compare various published translations.

The "minimal transfer" for Matthew 7:19-21 results in the following closest equivalent: [1]Every [2]tree that does [3]not [4]BEAR/BRING FORTH [6]good [5]fruit [7]is-cut-down/is-hewn-down [8]and [11]is-cast/is-thrown [9]into the [10]fire. [12]So/therefore [13]indeed [14]BY [17]their [15]* [16]fruits you [18]shall-know/shall-recognize [19]them. [20]Not [21-22-23]every-one-who-says

[24]to-me, [25]Lord, [26]Lord, [27]shall-enter [28]into [29]the [30]kingdom [31-32]OF HEAVEN, [33]but [34-35]the one who does [36]the [37]will [38]OF [40]my [39]Father [41]WHO-IS [42]in [43-44]HEAVEN.

In the minimal transfer underlining indicates words added for which the original has no counterpart. Words requiring an altering of the lexical meaning appear in all-capital letters. Asterisks mark the omission of words from the original text. Variations in the numerical sequence of words indicate changes in word order. Comparison of sentence structures reflects any changes in syntax.

(4) The next step allows a comparison of different English translations, one by one, with the closest equivalent translation of the section under consideration. The comparison reflects five types of differences: changes in word order, omissions from the text, lexical alterations, syntactical alterations, and additions to the text. Each time a translation differs from the closest equivalent translation, an appropriate numerical value is assigned, following the value of one for changes in order and omissions, two for lexical and syntactical alterations, and four for additions. The value depends upon the kind and degree of the difference between the closest equivalent and the version being investigated. The numerical total establishes a 'deviation value' for the section analyzed in that particular translation. From this deviation value for a given number of words, one can extrapolate a deviation value per one hundred words.

The following example compares Today's English Version with the closest equivalent for Matthew 7:9-21. The sequential numbers are assigned to the words and phrases in TEV to facilitate the comparison:

[1]Any [2]tree that does [3]not [4]BEAR [6]good [5]fruit [7]is-cut-down [8]and [(11)*] [11]thrown [9]IN the [10]fire. [12]So, then, [13*] you [18]will-know [19]THE-FALSE-PROPHETS [14]BY [15*] [16]THE-WAY

[17]THEY ACT. [20]Not [21-22-23]every-PERSON-who-CALLS [24]ME [25]Lord, [26]Lord, [27]will-enter [28]into [29]the [30]Kingdom [31-][32]OF HEAVEN, [33]but <u>only</u> [34-35]THOSE-WHO-DO [36*] [(37)]WHAT [40]my [39]FATHER [41*] [42]in [43-44]HEAVEN [37]WANTS <u>them</u> to do.

Following the procedure outlined above will result in the deviation value for this section of Today's English Version as shown in the chart below.

Difference	Number	Value	Totals
1. Changes in order	4	#18--1 #19--1 #17--2 #37--4	8
2. Omissions	5	#(11)--1 #13--1 #36--1 #38--1 #41--2	6
3. Lexical alterations	3	#19--2 #16--4 #21-22-23--1	7
4. Syntactical alterations	5	#17--4 #24--2 #34-35--1 #37--4 #39--4	15
5. Additions	3	#12-13--2 #33-34--2 after #37--8	12
GRAND TOTAL			48

A deviation value of 48 for a 44-word section is equivalent to a value of 108 per 100 words.

(5) The final step entails repeating the whole process for other passages to obtain a sufficient sampling of a given book of the Bible. The average of the deviation values from all the passages becomes the single deviation value per one hundred words for the whole book. That process is repeatable for each book of the Bible in a selected version.

The analysis may proceed one step further. If one wished to calculate a single deviation value for the whole of a translation, one could do so by averaging the values of the sixty-six books. That, of course, presupposes extensive research involving a sufficient number of representative passages from each of the books.

Deviation values obtained through the deviation test have little significance as absolute quantities, but when compared to each other, version by version, the versions closer to the original text are identifiable, as are the versions that differ more extensively from the original text.

From the relationship of these values to each other one can construct a diagram to reflect a profile of English translations. A range of deviation values for literal translations, free translations, and paraphrases is discernable to show where each translation falls within one of those categories as well as how each translation relates to the others. Such a diagram for the book of Romans appears in Figure 1 on the next page.

Evaluating the Techniques
The diagram in Figure 1 helps in measuring the relative deviations of translations from the original Hebrew and Greek texts, but it also reflects the purposes of the translators. The dominating concern for those translations lying in the range of literal translations was closeness to the original. Within that range are further degrees of literalness indicated by the nine versions found therein. The most literal of the seven is the American Standard Version (1901). Because of

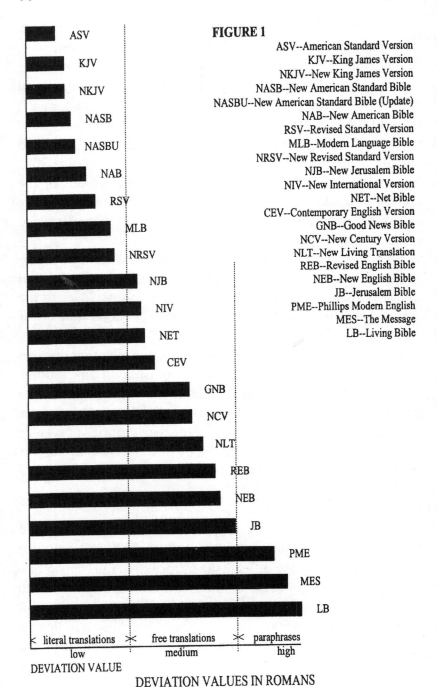

FIGURE 1

ASV--American Standard Version
KJV--King James Version
NKJV--New King James Version
NASB--New American Standard Bible
NASBU--New American Standard Bible (Update)
NAB--New American Bible
RSV--Revised Standard Version
MLB--Modern Language Bible
NRSV--New Revised Standard Version
NJB--New Jerusalem Bible
NIV--New International Version
NET--Net Bible
CEV--Contemporary English Version
GNB--Good News Bible
NCV--New Century Version
NLT--New Living Translation
REB--Revised English Bible
NEB--New English Bible
JB--Jerusalem Bible
PME--Phillips Modern English
MES--The Message
LB--Living Bible

ASV
KJV
NKJV
NASB
NASBU
NAB
RSV
MLB
NRSV
NJB
NIV
NET
CEV
GNB
NCV
NLT
REB
NEB
JB
PME
MES
LB

⊱ literal translations ⊱   free translations   ⊱ paraphrases
low   medium   high

DEVIATION VALUE

DEVIATION VALUES IN ROMANS

its literalness the ASV is the best English Bible for study purposes. Its disadvantage is that it retains an early style of English that is hard for some to comprehend (see the final chapter of this work, 'Types of English in Bible Translations,' for more discussion of English style). Study of any English translation can never replace study of the Bible in its original languages, of course, but the proximity of the ASV to the original makes it the best suited among English translations for this purpose, assuming, of course, that one understands Shakespearean English well. Other translations such as Darby's New Translation from the Original Languages and Young's Literal Translation are closer to the original than the ASV, but their diligence in allowing the original to dictate English wording and sentence structure makes their translations difficult for English readers to follow.

Moving to the right on the diagram in Figure 1, one reaches the range of free translations. These are works where a desire for readability has overshadowed the principle of closeness to the original. The New Jerusalem Bible and the New International Version mark where this range begins because the introduction of the latter says its purpose is not to produce an exact word-for-word translation. Since the NIV seeks primarily to translate ideas, not words, it clearly belongs among the free translations. The NET Bible which is very close in deviation value to the NIV and NJB calls itself a dynamic-equivalence translation. The proximity of the NJB to the original approximates that of the NIV and the NET, so the same is true of that translation. The New Revised Standard Version, on the other hand, with a deviation value somewhat lower than that of the NJB, the NIV, and the NET is probably close enough to the original to be categorized among the literal translations, but it is a close call.

Deviation values higher than that of the NJB and the NIV within the free translation range show less and less proximity to the original. The higher the values become, the more the translator's opinion in interpretive matters dominates. At the same time, however, the higher values usually mean more attention to user-friendliness in contemporary English.

At some point, however, the translated work becomes so free that it is best called a 'paraphrase'. The line of demarcation between free translations and paraphrases comes somewhere between the deviation value of the Jerusalem Bible and that of Phillips Modern English translation. The freeness of PME in rephrasing the text places it in the paraphrase category. Because of an even higher deviation value, The Message and the Living Bible are quite clearly best characterized as paraphrases. Paraphrases of the Bible are quite distant from the original and have the dominating objective of communicating effectively in the idiom of contemporary English.

The above comments regarding the Deviation Value Diagram highlight an advantage of literal translations that is badly lacking among free translations. A literal translation provides a reliable tool for *studying* the text, because it is close to the original text. The more remote a translation is from the original, the less it reflects the precise meaning of the original and the more it reflects the interpretations of the translator(s). That remoteness entails a hindrance if one's purpose is to discover the meaning of the Bible. The translator's interpretations loom larger in the translation in proportion to the amount of freedom exercised in the translation technique. The reason for this is that the translator chooses his own ideas about the meaning of the text to replace the literal rendering of the text. A student of Scripture usually seeks the meaning of the text, not an interpretation of the translator. If he wants someone's interpretation, he will consult commentaries on the text. Free translations and paraphrases are especially harmful where the translator has erred in his interpretation.

That misleads a student of the Bible as to what God actually said without the reader being aware that he is accepting someone's interpretation rather than what the original text says.

An extreme example of how a translator's misinterpretation may mislead an English reader is in Luke 16:9 of the Living Bible. That paraphrase transforms the verse into two questions that completely change the meaning of the Greek text. In the original Jesus commands his disciples to use mammon wisely: 'Make friends for yourselves by the mammon of unrighteousness that when it fails, they may receive you into everlasting tabernacles.' But the Living Bible turns the words into a prohibition against using mammon constructively: 'But shall I tell you to act that way, to buy friendship through cheating? Will this ensure your entry into an everlasting home in heaven?' (Incidentally, 'cheating' is not a good translation of the word for 'mammon'.) A footnote accompanies this change in an attempt to soften it, but the fact remains that the paraphrase has substituted what the translator thinks the text should say for what the original actually says and, in so doing, has obscured the passage's real meaning.

Other examples of how an English reader is at the mercy of the translator's interpretive decisions come from Galatians 5:12. The King James Version has a literal rendering: 'I would they were even cut off which trouble you.' What is meant by 'cut off' is a matter of debate. Readers of the Living Bible and Phillips Modern English paraphrases are shut up to the idea that it means separated from the Christian assembly; their renderings yield no other possible interpretation. Readers of the Revised Standard Version and the New Living Translation can opt only for a reference to the removal of some member of the human body in connection with the words 'cut off.' Nine free translations—Today's English

Version, New International Version, Jerusalem Bible, New Jerusalem Bible, New English Bible, Revised English Bible, The Message, The New Revised Standard Version, and New Century Version—interpret Paul's 'cut off' even more narrowly to refer to a depriving of the male reproductive glands.

The interpretations in some of these translations are wrong; they cannot all be right, because they contradict each other. If a reader depends on one that is wrong, he has no way of knowing that other options are open. The only safeguard against this possibility is a literal rendering such as is found in the KJV, one that does not commit itself to either of the varying alternatives. The student of the English rendering will then sense the ambiguity and search elsewhere to ascertain which of the alternative interpretations he should choose.

On the other side of the issue, the relative ease in reading made possible by free translations and paraphrases is a counterbalance that somewhat offsets the disadvantage encountered in using dynamic-equivalence products for interpretive purposes. Increased readability encourages the casual reader, one who reads for enjoyment and not so much from a motivation for substantive learning. Among such readers are non-Christians who may read a free translation or paraphrase because of the beauty of its literary style and, in the process of doing so, become believers in Christ as a result of what they read. Dynamic-equivalence translations are a good tool for evangelizing the lost.

The one who has not undertaken a translation project may ask why it is not possible to produce a literal translation that possesses the same kind of appealing English as is found in free translations and paraphrases. Such an easily readable, literal translation is impossible because of basic differences between the source languages and English. And even in the source languages, producing a striking literary effect was not the goal of much of the Bible. To create something in English that meets the criteria for smooth reading necessitates sacrificing something by way of closeness to the original.

The Final Choice
In settling upon one or the other of the philosophies of translation, one must sacrifice something. The question is, which sacrifice will hurt the least in the long run? Though individual preferences may vary, theological considerations dictate that closeness to the original must be the prime consideration, because God's seal of approval rests on that inspired text. If a literal translation is in reasonably smooth English, even though it may not be the most appealing in English style, the loss in communicative effectiveness is less than it would be through failing to have a translation that reflects the original text fully and accurately.

This is not to say that dynamic-equivalence translations do not have a place. They do. They are useful in specialized situations, but historically the English-speaking church has never made this type of translation its preference for general use, except perhaps for brief periods of time. The church will probably never do so on a permanent basis. The church needs as its mainstay a literal translation that will stand up under the close scrutiny of intensive study.

The serious Bible student also expects such proximity to the original languages of Scripture. That kind of translation can also serve the needs of a non-Christian and of a casual Christian whose use of the Bible, at least for a time, is more superficial, if the English style is good enough to be inoffensive. But there is also something to be said for recommending a free translation to someone until he becomes more intense in his thirst to study and learn the meaning of Scripture on his own. At that point he should be 'graduated' to a more literal English version as his source of study.

Selected Reading List

de Waard, J., and E. A. Nida. *From One language to Another, Functional Equivalence in Bible Translating.* Nashville: Nelson, 1986.

Glassman, *The Translation Debate—What Makes a Bible Translation Good?* Downers Grove: InterVarsity, 1981.

Jeske, C. 'Faculty Review of the Revised *NIV*,' Wisconsin Lutheran Quarterly 85/2 (Spring 1988): 106.

Kohlenberger, J. R., III. *Words about the Word—A Guide to Choosing and Using Your Bible.* Grand Rapids: Zondervan, 1987.

Kubo, Sakae, and Walter F. Specht. *So Many Versions?.* Revised Edition. Grand Rapids: Zondervan, 1983.

Lewis, Jack P. *The English Bible from KJV to NIV: A History and Evaluation.* 2nd ed. Grand Rapids: Baker, 1991.

Miller, E. L. 'The *New Internation Version* on the Prologue of John,' *Harvard Theological Review* 72/3-4 (July-October 1979): 309.

Nichols, A. H. 'Explicitness in Translation and the Westernization of Scripture," *Reformed Theological Review* 3 (September-December 1988): 78-88.

Nida, E. A. *Toward a Science of Translating, with Special Referenct to Principles and Procedures Involved in Bible Translating.* Leiden: Brill, 1964.

Scott, J. W. 'Dynamic Equivalence and Some Theological Problems in the *NIV*,' *Westminster Theological Journal* 48 (Fall 1986): 355.

Sheeley, Steven M., and Robert N. Nash, Jr. *The Bible in English Translation: An essential Guide.* Nashville: Abingdon, 1997.

Thomas, Robert L. 'Bible Translations: The Link between Exegesis and Expository Preaching,' *The Master's Seminary Journal* 1/1 (Spring 1990): 53-73.

_____. 'Dynamic Equivalence: A Method of Translation Or a System of Hermeneutics?' *The Master's Seminary Journal* 1/2 (Fall 1990): 149-175.

Wonderly, W. L. *Bible Translations for Popular Use.* London: United Bible Societies, 1968.

Chapter 4

THEOLOGICAL BIAS
IN BIBLE TRANSLATIONS

Theological prejudice is a strong influence in many realms, and Bible translation is one of those realms. Understanding its impact on Bible translations requires careful analysis, however, because it is easy to misrepresent theological bias in Bible translation.

Translation in itself is an objective activity in which it is difficult for a translator to distort to a large degree the literature he is translating. That is particularly true in translating the Bible. Translators may impose their own opinions on their versions occasionally, but it is very difficult for them to hide the true scriptural message in its broad impact even if they do misrepresent the text here and there.

A number of instances discussed below will reflect the partisan position represented by views of different translators. Yet the nature of the translation discipline is sufficiently objective to reduce to a minimum the overall impact of such bias. In other words, though the fruit of prejudice may be evident in a translation, it rarely affects the reader's broad conclusions about doctrine when doctrinal matters are studied in the broad scope of a whole translation. It may mislead him regarding a detail on a few occasions, but in almost every case he can formulate teachings that are generally sound.

Four methods of detecting theological bias present themselves. First, the theological viewpoints of the translators may be a matter of general knowledge. A translation sponsored by the Roman Catholic Church would reflect the views of that church body as the New World

Translation would support those of the Watchtower Bible and Tract Society. Translators unconnected with a large organization will have biases too. Any translator will endeavor to keep his opinions from influencing his translation, but inevitably his prejudices will be a determining factor in how he renders certain passages. Detecting theological bias by this method is much easier in translations by one person, because works done by committees usually reflect a mixture of views held by different members of a translation team. One or more of the three methods described below will often confirm conclusions derived from this kind of information.

A second way of detecting theological bias is through a statement or statements made in introductory materials found in the translations themselves. Occasionally translators will disclose their viewpoints on certain doctrines in these opening comments. That is especially the case in regard to the inspiration of Scripture. Sometimes inspiration itself will not be the main point of the discussion, but rather the technique (or philosophy) of translation as it relates to belief about inspiration. Those who believe in verbal inspiration of Scripture will often incline toward a literal (i.e., formal-equivalence) translation technique. Close attention to introductory matter will often result in discovery of these kinds of data.

Thirdly, notes that accompany a translation will often disclose doctrinal perspectives in the translation. The Geneva Bible furnishes an example that is well known for this. Produced under strong Calvinistic influence, the version and its notes proved to be very irritating to King James and some associated with him in translating the King James Version. They vowed that no such notes would appear in the KJV. Numerous illustrations of this type of procedure occur, as will be seen from some of the examples in the discussion to follow.

Such versions often print notes at the bottom of the same page as the Bible text, but sometimes they may be in the margin beside the text.

A fourth way for deriving information about theological prejudice lies in the text itself. The words of the translation are, after all is said and done, the heart of the issue. From them the reader can derive a variety of insights about the doctrinal preferences of translators. He must be cautious, however, in drawing conclusions from this type of resource, because sometimes a translator may conform to a given doctrinal pattern unconsciously. He may choose a rendering without realizing its theological implications. All translators are not theologians, so they cannot always foresee the nuances of meaning conveyed by various English expressions.

In spite of the necessary caution, however, this fourth area of theological investigation is most important. It provides the richest dividends, and so should not be slighted. The following discussion of different categories of doctrine will draw largely from it, but will also use the other three methods to enrich the discussion.

Of course, a discussion of theological prejudice in translation can only be suggestive. It cannot exhaust all the evidence of bias in all the translations. That would be a seemingly endless task. Principal focus will be on the New Testament, but occasional references to the Old Testament will provide a fuller coverage of the subject.

For convenience, the discussion will divide material into the major categories of Systematic Theology.

Bibliology (the Doctrine of Biblical Inspiration)

The viewpoints of translators about the Bible's inspiration are quite important. Their views have at least an indirect and possibly a direct bearing on how people handle the text they are translating. Comments of two earlier translators reflect that fact. Moffatt in the preface to his free translation justifies his translation methodology by declaring that he, along with others, had been 'freed from the influence of the theory of verbal inspiration' (James Moffatt, *The New Testament, A New Translation*, 1913, vii). He equated a word-for-word translation with an outdated view of verbal inspiration. In a similar vein Phillips, in the introduction to one of his paraphrases, wrote, '...Most people, however great their reverence for the New Testament may be, do not hold a word-by-word theory of inspiration...' (J. B. Phillips, *The Gospels Translated into Modern English*, 1952, v). He used this to justify his type of translation of the New Testament. By conservative theological standards those two viewpoints leave much to be desired, and raise questions about what kind of liberties the translators may have taken in view of their lower view of inspiration.

In contrast to these two works is the Foreword of the New American Standard Bible which states that the work '. . . has been produced with the conviction that the words of Scripture as originally penned in the Hebrew, Aramaic, and Greek were inspired by God'. The bias of this work lies on the side of verbal inspiration, a philosophy that shows itself in that version's philosophy of literal translation. The same is true of the New King James Version whose translators, in line with the version's policy of 'complete equivalence in translation', signed 'a statement affirming their belief in the verbal and plenary inspiration of Scripture, and in the inerrancy of the original autographs'.

Yet the correlation between a belief in biblical inerrancy and an adherence to formal equivalence in translation methodology is not without exception. The translators of the Revised Standard Version were more liberally oriented in regard to inspiration, and yet produced a literal translation. Conversely the translators of the New International Version were evangelical, but followed the dynamic-equivalence principle. The introduction to this work at one time during its development spoke disparagingly of formal equivalence, saying that it was 'based on a mistaken concept of human language' (Committee on Bible Translation, Preface to 'The Gospel According to John, A Contemporary Translation,' 1969; the name 'A Contemporary Translation' was later changed to 'The New International Version'). That wording has changed to the following in current editions of the NIV, saying the translators 'have striven for more than a word-for-word translation'. They have sought a meaning-for-meaning correspondence, which puts the work in the free-translation category. Yet the translators affirm their commitment 'to the full authority and complete trustworthiness of the Scriptures'.

So while free translations and paraphrases in their earlier examples are historically traceable to a loosened view of inspiration, a few translators who hold a high view of inspiration have followed dynamic-equivalence principles. They do not seem to realize the close tie-in of dynamic equivalence with a strong trend toward subjective hermeneutics and the implicit (sometimes explicit) relationship of subjectivity in hermeneutics with a lower view of inspiration. The free-translation philosophy shifts the control in translation from the original text to a variety of contemporary issues, allowing a translator to take great liberties in what he does with the text. Developing this topic further is not appropriate at this point, but readers may pursue it further by consulting my article 'Dynamic Equivalence: A Method of Translation Or a System of Hermeneutics?' that appears as an Appendix in this volume.

Another characteristic of translations that reflects the translators' views of inspiration is their handling of Old Testament prophecy and its New Testament fulfillment. The Revised Standard Version translators seemingly reflect a lower view of inspiration in this regard. In many cases that version obscures the relationship between the prediction and its fulfillment through its choice of renderings. Where legitimate options of rendering two passages the same exist, thereby demonstrating the supernaturalness of fulfilled prophecy, they have chosen to go different routes in the English. That results in a playing down of the continuity between the Old and New Testaments, and consequently a reduced evidence of the divine inspiration of the Bible.

One example of this non-correspondence is Psalm 45:6a. There the RSV has, 'Your divine throne endures for ever and ever.' In Hebrews 1:8a the writer professes to record a fulfillment of those words by the Son of God, but the RSV all but obscures the fulfillment when it gives, 'Thy throne, O God, is for ever and ever.' The Hebrew text legitimately permits the rendering of 'divine' in Psalm 45:6 as a vocative, 'O God.' Also the Hebrew for 'endures' is more accurately 'is'. The translators could have chosen such possibilities, and the correspondence with Hebrews 1:8 would have furnished an obvious fulfillment of prophecy. But they did not, perhaps because of a weak view of inspiration. Today's English Version conceals the prophecy-fulfillment relationship between these two verses in a similar way. On the other side of the issue, an example of a high view of inspiration is the Modern Language Bible. It renders both verses in an identical way: 'Thy throne, O God, is for ever and ever' (cf. also the NASB).

Another indicator of a weakening view of inspiration is the trend toward producing gender-neutral translations. Translations of this type have placed more weight on contemporary cultural preferences than they have on representing what was written when writers penned various books of the Bible. Not only does this policy increase a translation's deviation from the original texts, but it also raises questions about principles of interpreting those texts. It creates a false impression about the cultures in which the Bible first appeared. Gender-neutral translations purport to 'correct' the exclusion of women created by the patriarchal culture of biblical times by expanding male references in the text of Scripture to include females. Versions that have this as their purpose include the NCV, the NET, the REB, the NJB, the NLT, the NRSV, and the CEV. The inclusive-translation principle shows itself, for example, in the translation of the Greek word for 'brothers' by the expression 'brothers and sisters'. The pitfall of this policy lies in its failure to convey accurately the historical situation of the original. It attempts to bridge a contemporary cultural gap by misrepresenting what the writers wrote. If a translator obscures that cultural feature, what keeps him from obscuring other cultural features of the original text that contemporary cultural perspectives find distasteful?

The New Testament and Psalms: An Inclusive Version, published by Oxford Press in 1995, illustrates other areas of concession to contemporary culture. In its attempt to overcome other barriers to full inclusion of this group or that, the version seeks to avoid offending various oppressed minorities and disabled people with renderings such as 'enslaved people' instead of 'slaves', 'people with leprosy' instead of 'lepers', and 'blind people' instead of 'the blind'. Instead of references to God's 'right' hand as a place of privilege, it uses other terms to express power or nearness so as not to offend people who may be left-handed. That type of work goes beyond translation into subjectivism that presents what the translators think the Bible should say instead of what it actually says.

Christology (the Doctrine of Christ)
A study of how different versions have represented the person
of Christ is also revealing in regard to theological bias.
Sometimes renderings make His deity quite lucid, but at other
times the wording raises strong questions concerning whether
He is God.

Peter's well-known confession (Matthew 16:16) is an
instance that shows the difference. Some contemporary
English translations have used the old English second person
pronouns in language addressed to deity. Thus the RSV, the
NEB, the MLB, and the NASB contain 'thee', 'thou', 'thy',
and 'thine' numbers of times. Peter's words to Christ at
Caesarea-Philippi are a strong affirmation of Jesus' deity, so
one would expect '*Thou* art the Christ, the Son of the living
God' in these versions. Yet the MLB and the NASB are the
only ones that follow that pattern. By rendering the verse,
'You are the Christ,' the RSV and the NEB probably reflect a
lower view of Christ's person on the part of the majority of the
translators on their committees.

Romans 9:5 is also much discussed in connection with
Christology. The issue here is the manner in which to
punctuate the verse. If a full stop (i.e., a colon, semicolon, or
period) separates the name of Christ from the name 'God', the
statement affirms nothing regarding Christ's deity. The usual
punctuation of the verse, until the advent of some of the
twentieth-century versions, has been a half stop (comma) or
perhaps no punctuation at all. In fact, the majority of
twentieth-century translations has continued this usual
method, not making a strong separation between the two
proper names (John H. Skilton, 'Romans 9:5 in Modern
English Versions,' *The New Testament Student at Work*, vol.
2, 1975, 107-111). The exegetical evidence, though it has
been argued both ways, favors the half stop or no punctuation.
The verse is thus an explicit statement of the deity of Christ.

Some of the versions that support the deity of Christ in Romans 9:5 are the KJV, the ASV, the NASB, the NIV, the NJB, the NRSV, the NCV, the MES, the NET, and the JB. Among those that do not support the teaching of His deity in the verse are the LB, the NAB, the PME, the RSV, the TEV, the REB, the CEV, and the NEB. In this latter list it is surprising to find the LB because of the conservative theology of its translator. This is probably an instance of a translator not realizing the doctrinal implications of his rendering. The NLT has corrected this misrepresentation of the LB translator's beliefs about the person of Christ. The positions of the other works in both lists seem to agree with what is known of the theological inclinations of their producers.

Acts 20:28 is another testing ground for gauging a version's support of the deity of Christ. The Greek text reads as in the KJV, the NKJV, the NASB, the NIV, and others: 'the church of God which he purchased with his own blood' or a close equivalent of that. The words 'his own blood' refer back to 'God', furnishing a direct statement of the deity of Christ. The RSV avoids that direct statement, however, by adopting another reading that gives 'Lord' in place of 'God', thereby avoiding a clear statement of the deity of the Son. The NRSV recognizes that 'God' is the best supported reading in that verse by changing 'Lord' back to 'God' in Acts 20:28, but it has another way of avoiding a statement of Christ's deity. It reads 'the church of God that he obtained with the blood of his own Son'. In effect, it adds the word 'Son' to the text in order to find a way to avoid stating Christ's deity directly. The REB avoids advocating that Christ is God in a way similar to the RSV, and the NJB, the NCV, the TEV, and the NET shun the doctrine in essentially the same manner as the NRSV.

Most translations of John 1:1 state that 'the Word was God'. A few, however, vary from this. TEV has the Word 'was the same as God'. The NEB says, 'What God was, the

Word was.' These two versions are not as clearly explicit in expressing the deity of Christ, the Word, if they do so at all. The New World Translation predictably removes any reference to unique deity: 'The Word was a god.' One would not expect a translation effort sponsored by the Watchtower Bible and Tract Society, the publishing body of Jehovah's Witnesses, to support the deity of Christ. So the rendering in the NWT is no surprise.

TEV has a statement in Philippians 2:6 that is difficult and probably impossible to reconcile with the deity of Christ. It reads, 'He did not think that by force he should try to become equal with God.' That in essence appears to deny the Son's full deity by denying His equality with the Father. The rendering also happens to be a misleading representation of the Greek text on which it is supposedly based. The JB is more adequate with its words, 'he did not cling to his equality with God.' This latter rendering accepts that Jesus is fully God. The NJB is similar: 'Who, being in the form of God, did not count equality with God something to be grasped.' These last two versions bear the *Imprimatur* of the Roman Catholic Church, an organization that endorses the doctrine of Christ's deity.

Another illustration of Christological bias derives from the highly regarded ASV of 1901. A scholar of the Unitarian persuasion served on the translation committee for this work. Though greatly outnumbered by orthodox Trinitarians, he apparently left his mark in a note in the margin accompanying the word 'worshipped' in John 9:38. The note reads, 'The Greek word denotes an act of reverence, whether paid to a creature (as here) or to the Creator (see ch. 4, 20).' The blind man, having just come to faith in Jesus, 'worshipped' Him, but the explanatory note says Jesus is a mere creature. The note goes on to contrast Him with God the Creator in this respect. That is a rather explicit denial that Jesus is God. The

REB follows the same pattern. In John 4:20 they render the word by 'worship', but here in 9:38 it reads 'fell on his knees' rather than 'worshiped'. Similarly, the NEB renders 'bowed' in John 9:38 rather than 'worshiped'. Those renderings probably indicate a lower view of Christ's person.

Since the release of the RSV in 1952 much attention has focused on that version's rendering of 'young woman' in Isaiah 7:14. That version's failure to translate the prophecy by 'virgin' in agreement with Matthew 1:23 is probably indicative of the translators' hesitancy to see it as prophetic of Jesus' virgin birth. The NRSV translates the Isaiah passage the same way as do the NJB and the REB, raising the same questions about the theological biases of those translators.

Pneumatology (the Doctrine of the Holy Spirit)
The New World Translation displays the Jehovah's Witness denial of the personality and deity of the Holy Spirit by printing the word 'spirit' with a lower case 's' in each context where it refers to the Holy Spirit. Matthew 28:19 names the three persons of the Trinity, but the NWT has 'the name of the Father and of the Son and of the holy spirit'. Similarly in 2 Corinthians 13:14 it prints 'the undeserved kindness of the Lord Jesus Christ and the love of God and the sharing in the holy spirit'. Rationality for this procedure from a translator's viewpoint is impossible to fathom. Three names are in parallel with each other in the verses but only two of the three begin with capital letters, the third remaining uncapitalized. The phenomenon is traceable to the Watchtower organization's doctrinal bias.

One of the gifts of the Holy Spirit is the gift of tongues (1 Corinthians 12:10). The nature of this gift is disputed. Some understand it to be a species of ecstatic utterances incoherent to the human ear. Others view it as a miraculous ability to speak a foreign language different from one's own native language that may have been learned by natural means.

Translating the word for 'tongue' as simply 'tongue' leaves the English rendering noncommittal as to which interpretation is preferable. In 1 Corinthians 14 a number of versions have done this (e.g., NASB, PME, RSV, JB, REB, CEV, NJB, NET). Others, however, have decided to express one or the other of the viewpoints. The NEB explicitly indicates that the gift of tongues is a type of ecstatic speech. TEV less explicitly does the same when it calls the gift 'strange tongues'. Perhaps the NIV and NLT indicate a preference for this view when they use 'tongues' in the text and offer an alternative of 'other languages' and 'unknown languages' in their footnotes. Yet the NLT presents a mixed picture when in that chapter it in some instances uses 'unknown languages' in the text and 'tongues' as an alternative in a footnote. The CEV, the NIrV, and the NCV, on the other hand, consistently support the foreign language interpretation with their rendering of 'language(s)'. The LB joins these three in specifically teaching the foreign-language view when it translates speaking 'in tongues' with speaking 'in languages you haven't learned' (1 Corinthians 14:2). Neither of these interpretations necessarily indicates a Pentecostal or a non-Pentecostal orientation in a broader doctrinal sense. They simply illustrate how doctrinal bias may alter the designation of this aspect of the Holy Spirit's ministry.

Angelology (the Doctrine of Angels)
An unfortunate aspect of the KJV is its method of translating δαιμόνιον (*daimonion*), the Greek word for 'demon'. That version consistently confuses fallen angels, who are called 'demons' in the New Testament, with their leader, the devil. It refers to them as 'devils' throughout the New Testament. The effect is to keep the English reader from realizing that

there is only one devil but many demons.

A number of modern versions follow the KJV in this mistake. These include PME and the NEB. The JB does the same, but occasionally uses the accurate 'demons' in place of 'devils'. It is difficult to know the translators' reasoning for this erroneous policy. Possibly the practice reflects a disbelief in the existence of such spirit beings as angels.

Anthropology (the Doctrine of Man)
The NLT's introductory pages contain a section called 'Tyndale Bible Verse Finder' to help readers find Scriptures dealing with specific subjects. Among a number of human sins included in the list of subjects are two that reflect the translation's perspective on two contemporary issues that are controversial: abortion and homosexuality. The version's opposition to those two practices reflects its conservativism in comparison with those of liberal theological persuasions who find the two practices unobjectionable.

Soteriology (the Doctrine of Salvation)
The saving work of Christ on the cross is of supreme importance in Christian doctrine. How translations treat the subject reflects a good bit of their theology. For example, various translations have handled the doctrine of propitiation in different ways. That teaching involves the satisfaction of God's wrath against sinful man through the sacrifice of Christ. But some liberal theologians have taken issue with this rather clear teaching of the Bible, objecting to the idea that a God of love could also be a God of wrath.

To nullify that biblical teaching about God, some translators have substituted the word 'expiation' for 'propitiation' in a number of passages, because it eliminates the associated connotation of wrath found in the latter word (Romans 3:25; Hebrews 2:17; 1 John 2:2; 4:10). The RSV, the NEB, the NJB, and the REB are four that do this. Other versions leave something to be desired here too, by wording like 'the means by which our sins are forgiven' (1 John 4:10, TEV; cf. also the JB). The LB, on the other hand, very explicitly speaks of God's sending His Son 'to satisfy God's anger against our sins' (1 John 4:10). That reflects a conservative understanding of propitiation.

Another soteriological matter that divides translators of English versions is the security (or non-security) of the believer. Perhaps under some influence from the Geneva Bible, the KJV translators favored Calvinistic renderings in numbers of cases. They strongly rejected the Calvinistic notes of the Geneva work, but in spite of this seem to have used its expressions here and there in the text. In following Tyndale at Hebrews 6:6, the KJV leans toward the Calvinistic perspective with its 'if they fall away'. The RSV and the NIV in essence also adopt that rendering in facilitating a Calvinistic interpretation regarding the perseverance of the saints when they render same words by 'if they commit apostasy' and 'if they fall away', respectively.

The Arminian viewpoint shows its presence in this same verse in several versions. It comes in the form of an alternate translation offered in a footnote. Most translations use a causal word ('because', 'since', 'for') in the middle of the verse to connect the thoughts of recrucifying the Son of God and exposing him to public shame with the first part of the verse: i.e., 'because (or 'since' or 'for') they recrucify the Son of God and put him to an open shame'. These actions are causes of the impossibility expressed earlier in the sentence. The causal connection is very difficult for the Arminian perspective, however, since it leaves no opportunity for an apostate to be saved again. Therefore, in a footnote or marginal a few translations (the NASB, the NIV, and the NET) have offered a temporal word 'while' as an alternative for the causal conjunction. That allows the Arminian a way to avoid having the verse teach 'once lost, always lost'. The Arminian believes, of course, that if a person loses his salvation, he may through repentance regain it.

It is hard to avoid a Calvinistic rendering of Acts 13:48. Most versions accept the Greek as meaning that some are destined for eternal life (e.g., the KJV, PME, TEV, the NIV, the JB, the NEB, the NRSV, the CEV, the NJB, the NCV, the MES, the NLT, and the REB). But the LB very carefully avoids such a teaching in favor of one that makes eternal life dependent on the free will of man: 'As many as wanted eternal life, believed.' That translation does not represent the Greek text on which it allegedly rests.

Ecclesiology (the Doctrine of the Church)

Roman Catholic translations of Matthew 16:18 often have some type of note to support the view that Peter is the 'rock' on which Christ built the church. That is the case because of that organization's belief that Peter was the first pope of the Roman Catholic Church.

The New American Bible illustrates such a doctrinal inclination in its note on Matthew 16:16-20: 'To the tradition of Peter's confession at Caesarea Philippi (Mark 8:27-30), Matthew adds the doctrine of the divinity of Christ, together with Jesus' prophecy that he will successfully build a new Israel, i.e. the church, upon Peter.' Such would be expected, of course, in any translation bearing the *imprimatur* of officials of the Roman Catholic Church. This body would not sanction a translation that did not endorse its teaching about the papacy. That same note reflects the translators' inclination toward the Gospel writer's redaction of his traditional source (i.e., 'Matthew added') as well as their inclination toward a covenantal view of the church's replacement of Israel in God's program for His people (i.e., 'a new Israel').

Another work of this orientation is the Jerusalem Bible. It

indicates Peter's primacy in a different way, one that is a little
less direct. The note on 'Peter' in Matthew 16:18 says, 'Not,
until now, a proper name: Greek ... (*petros*) (as in English
saltpeter) represents Aramaic ... (*kepha*), rock.' Its note on
16:19 reads, 'The keys have become the traditional insignia of
Peter.' At Matthew 16:18 the New Jerusalem Bible adds
beside Peter's name the note, 'The name means "rock" ' to
support Peter's primacy. Surprisingly, The Message, in spite
of its evangelical Protestant origin, renders the verse, 'You
are Peter, a rock.' It was hardly the purpose of the translator in
this case to support the Roman Catholic view of the papacy,
however. The REB does essentially the same as The Message
with its rendering 'Peter, the Rock,' even though it is of
Protestant orientation.

In another phase of ecclesiology, how versions render
Galatians 6:16 is quite revealing. The KJV translates the
verse, 'And as many as walk according to this rule, peace be
on them, and mercy, and upon the Israel of God.' The
interpretive issue in the verse is whether 'the Israel of God' is
identical with 'them', the persons identified in the earlier part
of the verse. If the two are the same body, then the church and
Israel are the same, and the view of covenant theology that the
church has inherited the Old Testament promises to Israel is
correct. If the two groups in the verse are distinguished from
each other, however, the position of dispensationalism that
Israel and the church are separate peoples is correct.

Several translations have chosen to identify the two bodies
in the verse with each other, thereby displaying a preference
for the understanding of covenant theology. These include the
MLB, PME, the RSV, the NIV, the JB, the MES, the REB, the
NLT, and the NIrV. The LB, the TEV, the CEV, and the NEB
are less specific, but they lean the same way in their
implications. The NASB, the NAB, the NJB, the NRSV, and
the NCV, on the other hand, leave the matter ambiguous, as

does the KJV. This ambiguous rendering provides for either understanding, but it leaves the way open for separating the church from Israel, thereby recognizing two distinct peoples of God and providing for the customary dispensational interpretation. The NET is more explicit in supporting the dispensational approach: 'peace be on them—and mercy also on the Israel of God.'

Sometimes within the same translation conflicting theological prejudice will appear. This may be traceable either to a theological naiveté of the translators or to having different translators doing different parts of the translation. An interesting example of this is in the NEB. Acts 1:6 of this version sides decisively with the amillenarian camp of covenant theology when it transmits the disciples' question, 'Lord, is it at this time when you are to establish once again the sovereignty of Israel?' The Greek word behind 'sovereignty' is the usual word for 'kingdom'. There is an evident attempt to avoid a reference to a future kingdom for Israel such as is advocated by a premillennial dispensational approach. The NEB translator of Acts saw Israel's promise of a kingdom as fulfilled in the existence of the church.

The NEB translator of Ephesians, however, represented the other side of the issue (Ephesians 3:5). It may have been unwitting, but his translation is solidly on the dispensational side of a controversial issue: 'In former generations this was not disclosed to the human race; but now it has been revealed by inspiration to his dedicated apostles and prophets.' The LB, PME, the GNB, the NAB, the JB, and the NIrV do the same, i.e., categorically deny any previous revelation about Jews and Gentiles who are united in one body, the church. This denial is difficult, if not impossible, to reconcile with covenant theology's identification of the church as the new Israel. According to that system the Old Testament prophets foresaw the church when they delivered God's promises to

Israel. The REB follows the same pattern as the NEB both in Acts 1:6 and in Ephesians 3:5.

The RSV exemplifies another possible rendering of Ephesians 3:5: 'which was not made known to the sons of men in other generations as it has now been revealed to his holy apostles and prophets by the Spirit' (cf. also the KJV, the NASB, the MLB, and the NIV). Such a translation is ambiguous enough to allow that Old Testament prophets may have foreseen the church, but not to the same degree as revealed in Paul's day. Covenant theology can live with this much better than with the translations of those versions that categorically deny any previous revelation about Jews and Gentiles united in one body, the church.

A footnote in the NET at Acts 2:34 indicates the theological orientation of that translation toward a covenantal or progressive-dispensational view of the church. The note connects the word 'sit' in a quotation from Psalm 110:1 with a reference to the seating of the Messiah on David's throne in Acts 2:30, the implication being that Christ is currently seated on David's throne. The fulfillment of that role by Christ in the present rather than in the future fits with the view that the church is fulfilling Old Testament prophecies about Israel's future and has consequently in some sense replaced Israel thereby. That view conflicts with the distinction that dispensationalism makes between Israel and the church.

Eschatology (the Doctrine of Last Things)
In 1903 Richard Francis Weymouth published a New Testament designed to exclude theological and ecclesiastical bias. In his attempt for objectivity, however, Weymouth failed miserably, because his personal views regarding the state of the dead and the future life slipped through onto the pages of his translation. His translation of the frequent expression 'eternal life' was 'the life of the ages' because of

his inadequate understanding of the Hebrew idiom behind the expression. That misunderstanding has a direct bearing on the doctrine of soul sleep and eternal punishment. (A reviser later changed his unfortunate wording.) This same theological tendency characterized the Concordant New Testament (sixth edition, 1976). That version transliterates, not translates, the Greek word for 'eternal' and in a key-word concordance at the end of the version explains the transliterated term as referring to a limited period of time.

The Berkeley Version in Modern English (1960) displays its preference for amillennialism in a footnote relating to Revelation 20:6. It defines 'the first resurrection' of that verse as a spiritual resurrection by these words: 'Their spiritual resurrection had occurred as with all Christians at their regeneration.' This is the only way to reconcile the denial of a future millennial kingdom with the plain statements of Revelation 20 about the thousand-year reign of Christ. To suit their system of theology, amillennialists must make this reign coincide with the present era. In doing this, they posit two resurrections separated by a thousand years (they consider 'thousand' to be figurative), one being spiritual and the other physical. Premillennialists, of course, see both resurrections as physical, necessitating the doctrine of a future thousand-year kingdom. Revisers dropped that note in the revision of the Berkeley Version, now known as the Modern Language Bible.

The New King James Version in 2 Thessalonians 2:7 reflects a dispensational view of end-time events by capitalizing the pronoun 'He'. Since the version follows a policy of capitalizing pronouns referring to deity, that step reflects the translators' view that the restrainer in 2 Thessalonians 2 is God – probably the Holy Spirit – an understanding that coincides with a belief in the rapture of the church prior to the beginning of Daniel's seventieth week.

Summary and Choice

Most translators have striven to exclude their subjective opinions when producing English versions of the Bible. Hence, from any translation a person can derive a theology that is biblical in broad outline.

Yet no translation has successfully excluded doctrinal bias completely, and it is doubtful that one ever could. That factor compels the English-Bible user to exercise great theological discrimination in his choice of translations. In most cases he desires to choose a work whose views are the same as his own, and wisely so. His study of the Bible will profit much more if he does so, because he will not waste precious time and energy in weeding out translated portions that undermine or fail to support his own theological persuasions.

For example, if he believes in a verbally inspired Bible, he will want a Bible whose translators believed the same and produced a work as close to the original languages as possible. Or, if he accepts the full deity of Jesus Christ, he will want a translation that supports the teaching in the strongest possible way.

The same holds true regarding other doctrines. Certainly a person who believes in a God of wrath who will inflict eternal punishment on the lost does not want a Bible whose producers have sought to screen out allusions to God's wrath. Nor does a covenant theologian want to look to a version that excludes his system of theology in key passages.

The result of this discussion is not as clear-cut as we might like. One cannot recommend a translation that is best theologically for everyone, because people have different theological orientations.

What is possible, however, is to recognize works of a generally conservative outlook, since most serious Bible students view theological issues from a conservative perspective. Versions in contemporary English that fit this category include the NASB, the MLB, the NIV, the LB, the NLT, the NET, the NCV, and the MES. Among the older translations the KJV and the ASV are quite conservative in their perspectives. Other modern translations need to be used with care, if one wants to stay clear of liberal theological bias.

Selected Reading List

Bratcher, Robert G. 'The New International Version,' *The Word of God: A Guide to English Versions of the Bible*. Lloyd R. Bailey, ed.; Atlanta: John Knox, 1982.

Borowitz, Eugene B. 'Theological Issues in the New Torah Translation,' *Judaism* 26 (1975): 148-152.

Feinberg, Charles Lee. *The Revised Standard Version: What Kind of Translation?* Los Angeles: Bible Institute of Los Angeles, 1953.

Grudem, Wayne. *What's Wrong with Gender-Neutral Bible Translations?* Libertyville, Ill.: Coouncil on Biblical Manhood and Womanhood, 1997.

_____, and Grant Osborne. 'Do Inclusive-language Bibles Distort Scripture,' *Christianity Today* (October 27, 1997): 26-39.

Lewis, Jack P. *The English Bible from KJV to NIV: A History and Evaluation*. 2nd ed. Grand Rapids: Baker, 1991.

Metzger, Bruce M. 'The Jehovah's Witnesses and Jesus Christ: A Biblical and Theological Appraisal,' *Theology Today* 10 (1953): 65-85.

Sanders, James A. 'The Hermeneutics of Translation,' *Explorations: Rethinking Relationships Among Protestants, Catholics, and Jews* 12/2 (1998): 1.

Sheeley, Steven M., and Robert N. Nash, Jr. *The Bible in English Translation: An essential Guide*. Nashville: Abingdon, 1997.

Skilton, John H. 'Romans 9:5 in Modern English Versions,' *The New Testament Student at Work* 2 (1975): 107-111.

Thomas, Robert L. 'Dynamic Equivalence: A Method of

Translation Or a System of Hermeneutics,' *The Master's Seminary Journal* 1/2 (Fall 1990): 149-175.

_____. 'Holy Bible, New Revised Standard Version (a Review),' *The Master's Seminary Journal* 2/1 (Spring 1991): 111-115.

Chapter 5

TYPES OF ENGLISH IN
BIBLE TRANSLATIONS

Whether or not the English used in a translation suits a reader's taste will obviously influence that reader's choice of a Bible version. A surprising variety of English usage exists among English-speaking people of the world. Bible translations into English have not been exempt from the effects of this great variety. Translations currently available illustrate the many kinds of English that people use for communicating. Along with a discussion of classifications of English usage, this chapter on 'Types of English' will evaluate text formats and other miscellaneous indirect influences on English style.

Classifications of English Usage
Different types of English appear in both literal and free translations. It is true, however, that the philosophy of translation (see chapter 2 on 'The Techniques of Bible Translation') affects the kind of English to some extent. The original languages of Scripture place some limits on the patterns of language possible in literal translations, but even in those a translator has a degree of latitude to structure his work according to a particular linguistic style. A dynamic equivalence work, of course, has more freedom to accommodate itself to almost any English situation.

Though it is not the purpose of this discussion to exhaust the subject of English language usage—that is impossible because the subject covers the whole field of communications —a suggestive list of categories will stimulate thought about

the multiplied possibilities that prevail among the world's
English-speaking populations. Remarks will relate to ways
English has functioned in Bible translations. At least seven
kinds of factors are relevant.

1. Varying age levels. English used in addressing different
age-groups must differ if it is to communicate effectively.
This necessary variation arises from the obvious fact that in
the process of a lifetime each person's vocabulary and
grammatical habits change.

Children, for example, have limited vocabularies. The
Living Bible originated as an attempt to communicate
effectively with children. Kenneth N. Taylor produced it to
make the message plainer to his own children when the family
was reading the Bible and praying together. This work has
proven effective not only with children, but also with
teenagers and even with some adults. Its simplified approach
has appeal with all age-groups even though it originally
targeted the young.

Several other translations that have limited vocabularies
have seen effective use with children. Though designed for
those for whom English is a second language, such works can
also help others whose English vocabulary is limited because
of age. Two examples of this type of translation are The Bible
in Basic English, with a vocabulary of 850 English words, and
The New Testament: A New Translation in Plain English,
using 1,500 words plus 160 or 170 more that are found in a
glossary at the end of the book. S. H. Hooke completed the
former of these in 1949, and Charles Kingsley Williams the
latter in 1952.

The New Century Version, a version that was preceded in
lineage by the International Children's Bible (1986), is a more
recent work of this type. The NCV, like the ICB, limited its
vocabulary to words found in the *Living Word Vocabulary*, a

guide also used in compiling the *World Book Encyclopedia*.

'Large print' editions of various translations cater for the elderly who experience eyesight problems. They are a great boon for this age group, since otherwise they might have to curtail their use of Scripture prematurely. But interestingly younger children have found the large print helpful also, as they are learning to read. They profit from such editions during a span of several years while they are unaccustomed to smaller print-sizes.

Colored pictures spaced throughout both Testaments usually characterize children's Bibles. The pictures purpose to hold a child's interest while reading or being read to.

Literature tests have gauged the reading levels of several translations discussed in earlier chapters. The reading level indicated below represents the grade level of an average person to whom the translation is understandable.

Version	Reading Grade-Level
King James Version	12
New American Standard Bible	10
Living Bible	8
New American Bible	7
New Revised Standard Version	7
New King James Version	7
New International Version	7
New Living Translation	6
Contemporary English Version	5
The Message	5
International Children's Bible	4

It is apparent from the chart's reading-level figures that contemporary translations as a rule gear themselves to the elementary school level or slightly above. That means that most translations of this century are suitable for children.

2. *Varying stages of English language development.* The English language is constantly changing. Throughout its history it has never been static. Word meanings and grammatical customs continue in a state of flux. The best that any translation can hope for is to capture one of those stages of development that will give its text a relatively long public acceptance.

The King James Version is the prime example of a version whose English style has survived while many changes in English style and vocabulary have occurred. The English of this famous version represents what was in use at the time the translation came into being, or perhaps the type in use even a little before that translation was made. Word meanings and forms have changed many times since completion of the KJV, yet many still prefer its English style over three and a half centuries later. That is not because of its contemporary appropriateness, but because of the influence the version has exerted on the development of the English language. In the minds of a great number, for example, 'Thou' and 'Thee' are the only appropriate pronouns to use when addressing God in prayer, but these same modern-day people would never think of addressing another human being with anything other than 'you', never realizing that 'thou' and 'thee' were customary addresses in the day the KJV came into being. So great is this holdover influence that several recent versions that elsewhere use contemporary English have retained the old 'Thou' and 'Thee' in the language of prayer addressed to God (e.g., Revised Standard Version, Modern Language Bible, New English Bible, New American Standard Bible).

The reason usually given for continuing this custom is the connotation of reverence toward God that the older pronouns carry. This is probably true, but the distinction is purely one of English usage. The original languages' support for distinguishing 'thou' from 'you' in translating is nonexistent. The Hebrew, Aramaic, and Greek words behind both forms of the second-person pronoun are the same. Most of the versions that retained the older pronouns have now dropped them in their revised editions (e.g., the New King James Version, the New Revised Standard Version, the Revised English Bible, the New American Standard Bible [Updated]).

Because the English language is constantly changing, it is impossible to produce a translation whose English will remain contemporary. Word meanings change, idioms change, sentence structures change. Furthermore, the changes are completely unpredictable. They are the result of human whims in everyday conversation, making it impossible to anticipate them. For this reason, translators are dependent at best on an educated guess in their attempts to produce an English that will stand the test of time. How well they succeed rests on their ability to distinguish English usages that are just a passing fad from those that are more durable. Dynamic-equivalence translations (see chapter 3) are most susceptible to becoming outdated because their major focus is to communicate effectively by capturing contemporary idioms.

This has been evidenced toward the end of the twentieth century through revisions of several of them that have been prompted at least in part by changes in the English language since the release of the original versions. About twenty years after the appearance of Today's English Version (1976; i.e., the Good News Bible), the United Bible Societies followed it up with the Contemporary English Version (1995). The Revised English Bible (1989) came as a revision of the New English Bible (1970) after about the same time-lapse. The

New Jerusalem Bible (1986) followed the Jerusalem Bible (1967) after about nineteen years too. Twenty-five years elapsed between the Living Bible (1971) and the New Living Translation (1996).

Some translations, in trying to capture 'timeless' English, have retained language of the past. The Revised Standard Version, for example, has been criticized for such terminology as 'raiment', 'brethren', 'such an one', 'begone', 'smote', 'made a feast', 'took his journey', and 'made haste'. These are rarely used today. The NIV has examples of the same tendency: sometimes a woman is 'with child' rather than 'pregnant'; 'hallowed be your name'; 'debtors'; 'fishers of men'; 'a great company of the heavenly host'; and 'have not love'. Apparently in the judgment of the translators such expressions, though not up-to-date, have earned a permanent place in the vocabulary of Bible users, and they did not want to risk replacing them with contemporary language that might not meet with popular approval. An updating of expressions of this type may have in part prompted the revision of the RSV (1952) after thirty seven years (cf. the NRSV, 1989).

3. *Varying geographical locations.* The English spoken in different parts of the world varies. That is true not only within the United States where it is not too difficult to recognize regional differences, but also is characteristic of the English spoken in a number of different countries of the world. In the latter case the differences are much more pronounced than in the former.

For example, language differences between the United States and Great Britain are such as have hindered efforts to produce a version that is suitable for both sides of the Atlantic Ocean. The English Revised Version of 1885 was one such effort. A team of American scholars was invited to review the work of the English translators and to make suggestions for changes to 'Americanize' the work for the sake of United States readers. The English revisers found most of the American suggestions unacceptable, however. The solution to the dilemma was to allow publication of an American counterpart to the English Revised Version after a stipulated period of time. The result was the American Standard Version of 1901.

Another illustration of the geographical differences in English lies in a comparison between the work of James Moffatt, who published a New Testament in 1913 and an Old Testament in 1924, and that of Edgar J. Goodspeed who published his New Testament in 1923. Moffatt, a Scottish scholar, succeeded brilliantly in capturing the idiom of Scotland. Goodspeed, an American scholar, sought to produce an American translation that was free of English and Scottish expressions deemed strange to Americans. In the judgment of most he succeeded quite well in doing so.

The New English Bible offers frequent examples of this geographical phenomenon of language. Few Americans understand what is meant by 'Whitsuntide' (1 Corinthians 16:8), 'fell foul on him' (Matthew 13:57), 'midge' (Matthew 23:24), or 'widow's weeds' (Revelation 18:7). Yet these words and expressions find common usage in Great Britain.

The New International Version is another attempt to overcome this geographical obstacle. Scholars representing all the major English-speaking countries participated in this translation process in an attempt to avoid words and expressions that have only localized meanings. Yet the dominant leadership in the work came from the United States. Only time will tell how effective these efforts to find a 'worldwide' English have been.

The New Revised Standard Version has received praise for its particularity in expressing thoughts in *American* English. It will appeal to American readers more readily, but that does not mean it will have no appeal to those in other English-speaking countries. In contrast, the New English Bible has special appeal to readers in Great Britain because of it rather frequent 'Britishisms'.

4. *Varying amounts of education.* Amounts of education determine the kinds of English people use. Persons with more education develop vocabularies and styles of speech that differ from those with less education. The two groups are to some extent isolated from each other by their degrees of learning. Though communication between them is possible, each has a range of expressions that are beyond the comprehension of the other.

The more learned group unconsciously uses words that are commonplace to them, but of which the less learned have no knowledge. Likewise they draw upon technical terms and expressions and rhetorical devices with which the less learned are unfamiliar. At the other end of the scale the less learned use jargon and substandard vocabulary that is offensive, if not meaningless, to the learned. Further, their grammatical style is beyond the reach of those with more education than they have.

In the judgment of Wonderly, Phillips Modern English and the New English Bible at some points go beyond the reach of the less educated reader. Their styles and vocabularies are too sophisticated for him. An example of a version out of the reach of the highly educated class is the Cotton Patch Version of Paul's Epistles. Its language is often such as would repel an educated person. Wonderly suggests Today's English Version as an example of a version that lies within the range of both groups.

5. *Varying methods of communication.* Some translations are easier to understand when read aloud than others. It is true that a person usually comprehends what he sees in written form

better than what he listens to another person read. Therefore, audible comprehensibility deserves special consideration if translators anticipate their products will be read publicly.

Some translations do not lend themselves to public reading at all. The Amplified Bible, because of its frequent alternate translations and accumulations of synonyms, is one of these. It is also difficult to read aloud from a translation that has long sentences with infrequent punctuation.

The suitability of the King James Version for public reading is widely acknowledged. Its frequent punctuation marks facilitate this, but so do its prose rhythms. It appears that the KJV translators spent considerable time and effort in developing this aspect of the translation. That has greatly enhanced its communicative effectiveness for listeners.

Ephesians 1:3-14 is one sentence in the original Greek. The usual Greek punctuation of verses 3-10 has no colons or semicolons, only commas. That offers an intolerably long span of thoughts to be read aloud in English. The KJV has kept the whole section as one sentence, but has used a number of colons and semicolons to shorten the thought units. This is one solution to the difficulty. The New English Bible has broken the section into eight short sentences composing two paragraphs. The Revised English Bible does the same. The New Revised Standard Version has the same section in six sentences of one paragraph, but it also has one semicolon as an additional full-stop. These arrangements increase suitability for public reading. Another version notable for its short sentences is the New Century Version. That version divides Ephesians 1:3-14 into sixteen sentences.

The Contemporary English Version translators had as their major goal the producion of a version that could be read publicly. They divided Ephesians 1:3-14 into fourteen sentences. Their guiding principles were to make the text easy for an inexperienced reader to read aloud without stumbling, understandable to a hearer unfamiliar with traditional biblical terminology, and enjoyable to listen to because of a lucid and lyrical style. One example of how the CEV tried to accomplish these goals is in the way they handled poetry. Since most readers usually pause at the end of a line of poetry, they paid attention to line breaks in the text so as to reduce the possibility of the hearer misunderstanding what is read.

6. *Varying degrees of formality.* The classification of English according to functional varieties presents another category of English usage. Sometimes the language is formal, sometimes regular, sometimes casual, and sometimes intimate. No well-known Bible version has been produced in 'intimate' English, a style reserved for very personal situations. The casual style is the type used in personal letters. Today's English Version probably lies partially within this range. The Living Bible is more casual in its style than the TEV (i.e., GNB).

Phillips Modern English is a good example of the regular functional type. Its kind of communication represents that utilized in business correspondence. The level of formality is somewhat higher here than the casual category.

The formal class of English reaches a still higher level of formality. The New English Bible to some extent lies in this range, even though its purpose was to be a translation in 'newspaper' English. The language of the daily newspaper is more of a regular style. The NEB is best regarded as partially regular and partially formal.

Since the formal style is characteristic of articles written for learned journals, no translation would use this kind of English. Some do incline in that direction, however. The New International Version is one of these. Its tendency toward brevity gives evidence of this type of editorial attention in its production. Brevity of expression is one characteristic of formal writing.

Formality is not necessarily a drawback, however. Church congregations usually prefer some degree of this. It lends a dignity that most Christians view as quite appropriate for the Scriptures. The longer people are Christians, the greater their respect for the Bible. This outlook generally excludes preferences for translations that lack formality.

7. *Varying interests*. Many walks of life in the English-speaking world have mutual-interest groups. Each group has specialized terminology that is more or less 'foreign' to those outside the group. The special 'language within a language' may center around a sport or a hobby. Such expressions as 'middle voice', 'pertussis', 'mantissa', and 'disk drive' are common among specialists in the fields to which they belong, but to those unfamiliar with such areas of specialization the expressions have little or no meaning.

The same phenomenon comes into play in Bible translations. Some traditional biblical terms have little or no connotation for the unchurched person. Words like 'justification', 'sanctify', and 'propitiation' have meaning only for those who have had significant contact with Christianity and Christian teaching. The church is a special interest category with its own expressions that do not communicate to outsiders.

Such a factor poses another challenge to the translator. Should he design his work to communicate with the non-Christian or with the church-going Christian? Published versions of the Bible have answered that question both ways. The traditional versions such as the King James Version, of course, are quite appropriate within the church. So is the New American Standard Bible, a version shaped by English specialists who were pastors of churches. They served on the translation committee to help pass judgment on what English expressions the persons in the pew could or could not grasp.

Versions projected to communicate specifically with those outside the church include the Living Bible and Today's English Version. These have made a conscious attempt to remove the 'special interest' language that is unknown to those without extensive church contacts. They have incorporated substitutions for words such as 'justified' (Romans 5:1), 'reconciliation' (Romans 5:11), and 'propitiation' (Romans 3:25). Alternative renderings are not of a technical nature and are generally understandable by the average non-Christian.

A third group of translations seem to have a divided policy in this connection. Examples of this type include Phillips Modern English, The New International Version, and the New English Bible. They retain the more technical words in some places (e.g., Romans 5:1, 11), but offer less restrictive renderings in others (e.g., Romans 3:25).

The seven categories of English usage do not exhaust the subject, but with these seven in mind the reader can form a good opinion about how well each translation will meet his own needs in choosing which version to adopt.

Text Format
Other matters belong in a discussion of the varieties of English. The next general area is entitled 'text format'. Under such a heading come considerations of punctuation, capitalization, text arrangement, and print styles.

1. Punctuation. Perhaps the biggest punctuation difference between twentieth-century translations and those done before this century is the addition of quotation marks to the text. Quotation marks did not appear in versions up to and including the American Standard Version of 1901. Since then, most versions have incorporated them in appropriate places.

This is a welcome addition to the Bible text because it is customary in modern literature to indicate such things as direct quotations in this manner. But the use of quotation marks in the Bible text has not been without its problems. One of the difficulties is interpretive in nature. In some texts the translator must draw interpretive conclusions before placing quotation marks. A well-known case of this comes in John 3, whether to end Jesus' words at John 3:15 and understand verses 16-21 as comments of the writer John, or to continue Jesus' words through verse 21. The Revised Standard Version, for example, ends the quotation at verse 15, but the JB, the NEB, the NIV, the REB, the NJB, and the NRSV continue it through verse 21. Today's English Version offers another alternative, that of stopping the quotation at the end of verse 13. A version that uses no quotation marks does not have to take a position on this matter, and can leave the issue ambiguous as to where Jesus stopped speaking.

First Corinthians 6:12 reflects another interpretive decision necessitated by the use of quotations marks. The GNB, the NIV, the RSV, the JB, the NEB, the NRSV, the CEV, the NCV, the NLT, the NET, and the NJB place their equivalents of 'All things are lawful for me' in quotes because they take this to be a slogan well-known among the Corinthians. The NASB, the LB, the NKJV, PME, and the MLB do not understand the words in that manner, but take them as a plain statement of Paul. They therefore have no punctuation indicating a quotation.

A further problem that arises in the use of quotation marks is the situation of quotations within quotations. The Bible has frequent instances of not only quotations within quotations, but contexts where this phenomenon is tripled and even quadrupled. Such passages can become quite complex, as in the New American Standard Bible at Isaiah 36:10, where four sets of quotation marks appear consecutively. The verse concludes with a single quote, double quote, single quote, and double quote (i.e., ' " ' ").

All in all, however, the inclusion of quotation marks has proven beneficial to Bible readers, even though at times they require incorporating more translator-interpretation than would be necessary without them.

2. Capitalization. English versions traditionally have not capitalized the first letters of pronouns referring to deity. Because of the custom in some forms of modern writing to capitalize such pronouns, however, several versions have done so. Four which have are the Modern Language Bible, the New American Standard Bible, the New King James Version, and the New American Standard Bible (Updated).

This policy of capitalization is not without its problems. For instance, it may reflect an incorrect intent on the part of a speaker. In the MLB rendering of John 8:13, 'Yourself' and 'Your' are capitalized because they are pronouns referring to Christ. Yet the speakers of the words are Jesus' enemies, the Pharisees, who were not attributing deity to Him in the passage. They were, in fact, vigorously denying it. So though capitalizing pronouns referring to God may work well much of the time, it may in some cases give the wrong impression of a biblical character's estimate of Jesus. It actually reflects the translator's estimate.

Messianic prophecies of the Old Testament present another difficulty in the procedure of capitalizing pronouns referring to God. The policy is difficult to implement with consistency. The NASB capitalizes pronouns referring to deity in Psalms 2:7-9 and 45:1-17, but in Genesis 3:15 'him' refers to Messiah and is not capitalized. The NASBU follows the same inconsistent capitalization policy. The MLB does the same in the Psalms passages, but in Genesis 3:15 it is inconsistent within the same verse where it capitalized 'He', presumably because of its Messianic reference, and begins 'his' with a lower case letter.

Such difficulties as these have prompted most twentieth century versions not to follow the policy of capitalizing pronouns.

3. Text Arrangement. A long-standing debate that is yet unsettled to the satisfaction of all parties, concerns whether to print the Bible with the beginning of each verse on a new line or to group material thematically in paragraphs. The latter mode, it is argued by its proponents, follows the format of all other English literature. So why not treat the Bible text the same? Besides this, the verse-divisions and even the chapter-divisions are not always accurately placed. Coming at inopportune points, such divisions of the text disrupt thought-flow in a passage.

So goes the reasoning of those who prefer paragraph divisions. The reasoning has merit and is persuasive, as evidenced by the large number of modern translations that have chosen the paragraph format (e.g., PME, RSV, MLB, GNB, NIV, JB, NEB, NAB, NRSV, REB, NJB, NCV, CEV, MES, NKJV). Even some modern printings of the KJV arrange the text in paragraph form.

But tradition is a powerful argument too. Many, perhaps most, regular church-goers prefer beginning each new verse on its own line. It is difficult to assign a reason for this. Probably it is attributable to the pattern established by the King James Version. A long-standing habit is hard to break. Beyond this, however, is the ease of locating a verse with the verse numbers always at the left margin, as they are in the separate-verse format. No matter how ingenious the arrangement of type faces may be, it is inevitably more difficult to find a verse number buried in the middle of a paragraph. For these and perhaps other reasons, a few recent versions have retained the older form of text arrangement (e.g., Amplified Bible, NASB, NASBU).

An innovation that is common to practically all modern versions, whether they set the text in paragraphs or separate verses, is the way of typesetting poetic sections. Universally, or practically universally, it has become the custom to indent poetic sections of Scripture, such as the Psalms, with each line of the 'poem' placed on a line by itself. This has great advantage in showing the parallelism that exists in these passages of poetry.

4. Print Styles. One other aspect of text format deserves mention, and that is print styles. For purposes of this discussion 'print styles' refers to the use of italic letters in some Bibles to highlight English words that do not translate specific Hebrew or Greek words. The sense of the original implies such words as these though they are not explicitly expressed. The English sense requires them in order to make the English readable.

The Geneva Bible (1560) was the first to adopt this policy. The King James Version (1611) and the American Standard Version (1901) (cf. also the English Revised Version, 1885) followed that leadership. The Revised Standard Version and the New King James Version, though revisions of earlier works that used italics in this manner, have dropped the policy. The New American Standard Bible and the New American Standard Bible (Updated) are alone among recent major versions in retaining the use of italics for words not specifically supported by the original.

The disadvantage of using italic letters for unexpressed words is that it violates the usual significance of italics. In modern practice that type style normally indicates emphasis, but using it for words unexpressed in the original is supposed to convey a sort of de-emphasis. The advantage of using italics, on the other hand, lies in providing a means for the English reader to appreciate more fully what the original text behind a translation explicitly includes.

The New International Version has followed a similar policy for words not in the original text but required by the context. Instead of using italics to indicate such words, that translation encloses the words in brackets. Those brackets are relatively rare in the NIV, however.

The practice of using italics or brackets for the purpose of singling out words that are only implied is declining. Most translators judge that an implication of the original is sufficient to justify the presence of such words and to express them in the corresponding English rendering without special indicators. The original need not explicitly state the word or words.

Miscellaneous Influences on English Style

Several other aspects of English style are significant enough to warrant their mention. English style may to some extent be a reflection of a translation policy, of an individual who translated, or of the influence from a source language.

1. Translation Policy. Two extremes in translation policy exist. One extreme is to incorporate as much variety of English usage as possible. This perspective attributes much merit to variety in English vocabulary, whether it be to honor as many English words as possible by giving them a place in the Bible—a sentiment expressed by the translators of the King James Version—or to make the literary style as pleasing as possible for readers and listeners. Achievement of literary excellence by the KJV is unquestioned. Its widespread popularity over a period of almost four centuries is an eloquent testimonial to that fact.

Yet the very variety that makes the version so effective as a literary masterpiece has its disadvantages. It obscures from the English reader some of the principal emphases of the original text by taking several occurrences of the same Greek (or Hebrew) word in a given context and rendering it by a variety of English terms.

Two passages where varying the English vocabulary illustrates a loss of the emphasis in the original exemplify this disadvantage. In James 2:2-3 the Greek word *esthēs*, (garment) occurs three times. The KJV translates that Greek word by three different English words in the two verses: 'apparel', 'raiment', and 'clothing'. A student of the English text will thus probably erroneously assume that three separate Greek words lie behind the three English words. Another passage which illustrates this practice is 1 John 2:14-24 where the Greek word *menō* (I remain) occurs six times (vv. 14, 17, 19, 24 [3 times]). The NEB translates the six occurrences of the word by five different English words: 'remains', 'stands', 'stayed', 'dwell(s)', and 'keep'. The NIV translates the first two by 'lives' and three of the last four by 'remain(s)'. It leaves the sixth occurrence untranslated. That policy also obscures a prominent emphasis of the text.

The procedure cited in the above illustrations conceals a significant point the biblical writer sought to make. For that reason, some translators have adopted the other extreme of always rendering a Greek word by the same English word, the so-called 'concordant' approach. When followed to the limit, this method is an unrealistic view of the translation process. No two languages are so similar that a word in one has the same range of meanings as a word in the other. Contexts in which a Greek word appears determine which English words best translate it. Rarely does the same English word 'fit' in every context. On the other hand, the concordant approach is quite valid if the same Greek word occurs repeatedly in the same context.

For example, in James 2:2-3 the ASV renders *esthēs*

(garment) by the same English word, 'clothing', all three times it occurs. In 1 John 2:14-24 this same version renders *menō* (I remain) by 'abide(th)' five times and by 'continued' once. The Concordant Literal New Testament translates the same Greek word in 1 John 2:14-24 by some form of the word 'remain' in all six of its occurrences. The advantage of this type of consistency for a student of the English text is quite obvious. This latter work, the Concordant Literal New Testament, has carried the concordant approach to an unfortunate extreme in many of its passages. It has assumed more linguistic correspondence between Greek and English than actually exists.

The ASV in following the concordant method in a more balanced way has become a study tool for the English reader that is probably unsurpassed to the time of this writing. But it has lost the literary appeal of the KJV of which it was a revision. In the minds of many this loss explains the failure of the ASV to gain any kind of wide acceptance during the twentieth century. The first revision of it, the Revised Standard Version, returned somewhat to the policy of English variety found in the KJV.

A good resolution of the issue is that a balance between these two extremes is most desirable. It is precarious to name a translation that best represents such balance between variety and concordance, but if one were to venture an opinion, perhaps the NASB comes as close as any work presently available to striking that balance.

2. The Individual Who Translated. English style also reflects habits of the person (or persons) who translated. Nowhere is this more evident than in translations where diffferent people worked on different books or groups of books. Even though a central committee of some sort may review individual contributions, it is inevitable that the tastes of each contributing unit will be distinguishable in his work. That committee cannot completely undo the proclivities of whoever did the original draft without redoing the entirety of his work.

An interesting example of this comes from the NEB. Five times that version in Matthew 19:12 handles the Greek root from which the English word 'eunuch' comes. The NEB translator of Matthew, evidently feeling that the word is not common in modern times, decided against the use of the English word 'eunuch' and used equivalent expressions such as 'incapable of marriage' and 'renounced marriage'. In Galatians 5:12 of the same version, however, where the Greek root behind 'eunuch' does not appear, another translator has introduced 'eunuch' into the text: 'As for these agitators, they had better go the whole way and make eunuchs of themselves.' In the opinion of the Galatians translator 'eunuch' does enjoy common enough usage in modern English to justify its inclusion. Thus an inconsistency in English usage became part of the NEB translation. The REB follows the same pattern of inconsistency in the same two passages.

Inconsistency plagues any translation produced by different personnel working on different portions of the Bible. That is one of the main drawbacks of the Old Testament of the Berkeley Version (1959), one that to some extent has been overcome in a revision which has been named the Modern Language Bible. A difference in translators explains the varying quality of the Jerusalem Bible which in 1 Corinthians is a much more literal translation than in Romans. That same version is not consistent with itself in lexical choices. In Matthew and Mark the soldiers at the cross cast 'lots', but in John they 'throw dice' (Matthew 27:35; Mark 15:24; John 19:24), an inconsistency that the NJB has corrected. The same Hebrew word is rendered 'sandals' in Deuteronomy 29:4 and 'shoes' in Exodus 3:5, inconsistency that has been resolved by the REB. Also in the JB the body of water traditionally called the Red Sea is called both the 'Sea of Reeds' (Exodus 10:19; 13:18) and the 'Sea of Suph' (Numbers 14:25; Deuteronomy 1:40; 2:1), though the Hebrew expression is the same in all those passages. The NJB has not corrected that inconsistency of the JB. Examples of this type are common.

Though consistency is hard to obtain with multiple translators, another problem emerges if there is but one translator for a version. When one person does the entire work, his personal prejudices and peculiarities become magnified. Most acknowledge that those are more objectionable than a lack of consistency because of multiple translators. If a translator has a pet doctrine or a favorite unusual interpretation, he will tend to see his point of view in many passages, even in some where the pet issue is not relevant. Furthermore, various ramifications of different forms of English expressions will not occur to one person as frequently as they do to a team of translators. A translator needs the reactions of others to gain a well-rounded opinion of what each rendering suggests to the mind of a reader. Because of this it is doubtful that any one-person translation of the Bible will ever gain wide acceptance for more than a brief period of time.

The background of whether a translation has singular or plural translators has its impact on the English style of Bible translations.

3. *Influence of Source Languages.* Taking into account the influence of source languages is another consideration affecting English style. Translators stand in constant jeopardy of allowing their translations to be drawn into some stylistic pattern of the source language that is uncommon or even unused in twentieth-century English. If a translation does this,

common parlance applies the term 'wooden' to it.

Examples of this 'woodenness' in the KJV include such features as the bringing into English of the Hebrew idiom behind 'in blessing I will bless thee' (Genesis 22:17). Also the elongated sentence of Ephesians 1:3-14 in that version belongs to first-century Koine Greek, not to seventeenth-century English.

Some have called the NASB 'wooden' because of such things as its attempt to capture the nuance of meaning in the Greek imperfect tense. Its woodenness is mild in comparison with some others, however. Charles B. Williams did the same with all the Greek verbs in The New Testament in the Language of the People in 1937. This has caused the description 'prosaic and flat-footed' to be applied to that version. Kenneth S. Wuest's Expanded Translation of the New Testament (1956-59) attempted to do for all parts of speech what Williams did for the verb. Wuest's work contains such cumbersome English that it defies stylistic evaluation. J. N. Darby's The Holy Scriptures, A New Translation from the Original Languages is another work whose English has suffered heavily from distortion in the direction of the source languages.

The ideal, of course, is to eliminate such distortion without surrendering faithfulness to the original text if at all possible.

The above survey of the varieties of English has touched many facets as it has outlined the classifications of English usage, page format, and miscellaneous influences on English style. The numerous possibilities for differing patterns of style show the great challenge facing a Bible translator. The whole field of communications, with all its complexities, offers a challenge he must overcome. English-speaking peoples should be grateful for the high degree of success attained in many English translations of the Bible.

Selected Reading List

Kubo, Sakae, and Walter F. Specht. *So Many Versions?*. Revised Edition. Grand Rapids: Zondervan, 1983.

Lewis, Jack P. *The English Bible from KJV to NIV: A History and Evaluation*. 2nd ed. Grand Rapids: Baker, 1991.

New Living Translation: Holy Bible. Wheaton, Ill.: Tyndale House, 1996.

Nida, E. A., J. P. Louw, A. H. Snyman, and J. V. W. Cronje, *Style and Discourse*. Cape Town: Bible Society, 1983. 145-171.

Nida, Eugene A., and Charles R. Taber. *The Theory and Practice of Translation*. Leiden: Brill, 1969. 120-162.

Sheeley, Steven M., and Robert N. Nash, Jr. *The Bible in English Translation: An essential Guide*. Nashville: Abingdon, 1997.

Wonderly, William L. *Bible Translations for Popular Use*. London: United Bible Societies, 1968.

CONCLUSIONS

The survey of five areas for evaluating English Bible translations has shown the advantages and disadvantages of various versions. Among other things it has demonstrated that no perfect English translation of the Bible is in existence. This is probably disappointing to many who are seeking to find one version that will serve all purposes. All the versions have weaknesses, some more than others, but all have them. At this point a summary of a few strengths and weaknesses of the major versions is in order to illustrate how categories of evaluation apply to each.

Two limitations of this summary are noteworthy. First, a satisfactory evaluation of each version is difficult because different people have different goals and ideas about what they look for in a Bible translation. They have different ideas about what they value highest when looking for a translation to use. For example, a version that is easily readable is the highest priority for some, but others prefer one that is closer to the original texts of Scripture. Second, since this is only a *guide*, a comprehensive discussion of each version is impossible. The purpose of this work is to highlight *categories* for investigation, not to major in fulness of discussion about any single version. A full volume could devote itself to discussing characteristics of each of the major versions. An exhaustive treatment of all the versions would require a multivolume set of books. By focusing upon categories, this book has hopefully pointed out areas for each individual to investigate in settling upon his choice of a Bible translation.

In the following brief comments about the major versions selected for discussion, categories of discussion will follow

the chapter topics of this work: Chapter 1, Historical
Backgrounds (#1); Chapter 2, Textual Bases (#2); Chapter 3,
Methodological Techniques (#3); Chapter 4, Theological
Bias (#4); Chapter 5, Types of English (#5). A reader may
supplement the brief comments in this summary by
consulting an entry referring to each version in the Index of
Subjects at the end of this volume and turning to pages which
contain additional comments about that version.

King James Version
The KJV receives high marks for its role in the developing
lineage of the Tyndale tradition (#1). It capitalized on the
excellence of Tyndale's work and kept alive a sound
translation that served the church well for several centuries. It
also followed a philosophy of translation (#3) that valued
staying as close to the original text as the English language
would permit, and did so without doing disservice to the
English language. That version is also valuable because of its
conservative evangelical theological bias (#4). No errant
doctrinal views affected the translators significantly. It
furthermore has earned its place in history because of the
excellence of English style found therein (#5). Some might
choose to give it a lower grade because it has verse divisions
rather than paragraph divisions or because its English is not
contemporary (#5). A further disadvantage of the KJV for
study purposes is the varying of English vocabulary for the
same Greek word in the same context (#5). In the eyes of most
the major problem with the KJV, however, lies in its textual
basis (#2). General consensus is that the most accurate
manuscripts were not available in the days the translation was
made, forcing the translators to use an inferior Greek text in
the New Testament as a basis for the translation.

The New King James Version

The NKJV receives roughly the same marks as the KJV. It holds a later place in the Tyndale tradition than the KJV, but is still a part of the tradition (#1). It has the same philosophy of translation that makes it advantageous as a study tool (#3). The NKJV also has a conservative theological bias that those of an evangelical persuasion would prefer (#4). In English style it rates above the KJV because it uses contemporary English rather than Elizabethan English (#5). It also has altered the KJV proclivity of honoring as many English words as possible by giving them a place in the Bible (#5). That improves its usefulness for study purposes. Yet, the NKJV has the same problems as does the KJV regarding its textual basis, having chosen to remain with the *Textus Receptus* as its foundation in the New Testament (#2).

American Standard Version

The ASV lies in a good historical traditional as one of the descendants of the Tyndale translation (#1). It upgrades that tradition in the New Testament, however, by altering the textual basis to include manuscripts of a better quality and earlier date (#2). Its methodological technique of translation is the best for purposes of study in remaining as close to the original as possible without violating good English style (#3). It has some weaknesses in regard to theological bias for evangelicals, however, in raising occasional questions regarding the deity of Christ (John 9:38 [note]) and the inspiration of all Scripture (2 Tim 3:16) (#4), but overall its theological stance is of a conservative, evangelical posture. Its weakest area of all is its English usage, because it uses outdated English and because it gives too little consideration to literary style (#5). That last disadvantage is partly the outworking of the version's objective of being as close to the original as possible. The issue of English style, more than anything else, worked against the ASV obtaining widespread acceptance.

The Revised Standard Version

As a revision of the ASV, the RSV is a part of the rich historical lineage of mainline English Bible translations (#1). Another of its strengths is its textual basis, that of the generally accepted textual tradition (#2). Its translation methodology is also in the traditional mold; it is a formal equivalence translation (#3). It ranks higher than the NASB in readability because of its varying of vocabulary (#5), but that also is a disadvantage for its use as a study tool (#5). The major problem with the RSV for evangelicals is its theological bias, where it reflects a theologically liberal bias in relation to such doctrines as the inspiration of Scripture and the deity of Christ (#4).

New American Standard Bible

Historically, the NASB gets favorable marks because it falls in the Tyndale tradition (#1). It also ranks well for following a textual basis that is rated highest by most authorities (#2). The NASB also adopted a traditional or classical philosophy of literal translation (#3). It is a formal-equivalence or, as some call it, a verbal translation. The doctrinal environment under which it was produced is conservative, another strong point for evangelicals (#4). Yet the NASB rates low in the eyes of many because of its English style (#5). It has often been termed a 'wooden' translation because of this. That 'woodenness' results from two of its unique characteristics: the literality of its translation philosophy (#3) and its policy of translating the same Greek word by the same English word in a given context whenever possible (#5). Those two features, though detracting from its English style, are the very things that make the NASB one of the best study tools among modern translations.

New Revised Standard Version

The NRSV, like its predecessor, lies in the tradition of William Tyndale (#1). On the whole, its textual basis is sound because it traces back to the earliest and most reliable manuscripts (#2). The translation technique of the NRSV, however, has moved in the direction of dynamic equivalence as compared with the RSV, though it still lies in the broad range of literal translations (#3). The effort of its translators to produce a gender-neutral translation is largely responsible for that. The English style of the NRSV is pleasing (#5); although not as appealing as that of a number of the dynamic-equivalence translations. As with the RSV, the largest deficiency of the NRSV is theological (#4). The version is relatively weak particularly in the areas of Bibliology and Christology.

New American Standard Bible (Updated)

The NASBU differs from the NASB in only a couple of ways. One is in regard to its technique of translation. It has moved toward the dynamic-equivalence philosophy of translation because it omits numbers of conjunctions and shows more of a departure from the original than does the NASB (#3). The NASBU is still within the range of literal translations, but those changes reduce its effectiveness for study purposes. The other difference results from the same changes and produces an improvement in the style of English (#5), but the changes do not raise the level of readability of the NASBU substantially. In the judgment of most, it is still 'wooden'. The NASBU still enjoys the advantage of the Tyndale lineage (#1), of a sound textual basis (#2), and of a conservative theological stance (#3).

New English Bible

The NEB rates high in its English usage for those in Great Britain (#5), but not so high with American readers because of its 'Britishisms'. Its textual basis is generally strong but mixed, because in various places the translators chose readings that enjoy only weak support among the Greek manuscripts (#2). Its translation techniques find favor with those who prefer the dynamic (or functional)-equivalence approach (#3), an approach that reduces the version's usefulness for serious study. A question exists about its theological bias; it comes across as being liberal in some of the doctrinal areas (#4). Its historical background is practically nonexistent in comparison with the Tyndale tradition (#1).

The Revised English Bible

As a descendant of the New English Bible, the REB shares its very short historical lineage (#1). In addition to inheriting the Christological problems of the NEB, the REB compounds its negative theological bias by adding the bibliological problem stemming from trying to produce an all-inclusive—i.e., gender-neutral—translation (#4). The English style of the REB is good by virtue of its dynamic-equivalence approach that releases it from the grammatical patterns of the original text (#3), and by virtue of its decision to follow the KJV pattern of not having to render the same Greek word everywhere in the same context by the same English word (#5). The translation technique of the REB is that of a free translation (#3), a factor favored by the casual reader but viewed negatively by the serious Bible student.

New International Version

The NIV ranks highest in its English usage, according to most published opinions (#5). Many English readers find it quite easy to read. Its textual basis is the mainstream Alexandrian for the most part, though its textual basis is somewhat eclectic (#2). That means it did not follow consistently any one textual tradition. Its theological bias is unquestionably evangelical since it drew its translators from the ranks of evangelical scholars (#4). At one point in the recent past the NIV's producers were undertaking a gender-neutral revision of that version, but they halted the process when confronted with strong opposition from the evangelical community. If the effort to complete such a revision had succeeded, that would have been a serious bibliological drawback for the version. If free translation is a person's preference, he will like it for that reason too, yet this type of translation leaves much to be desired for serious Bible study of the English text (#3). The version is separate from the mainline tradition of English translations and therefore has no historical lineage (#1). The last two areas (i.e., #3 and #1) are the version's most serious weaknesses.

New American Bible

The NAB has a Roman Catholic theological orientation, which poses a serious problem for those of other doctrinal persuasions (#4). That means that Protestant readers cannot in some instances trust the version. The version has done as good a job of combining formal equivalence in translation (#3) with smooth English usage (#5) as any other English translation. It embodies a rare combination of readability and suitability for study. Its textual basis is sound, the NAB in its initial form being one of the earliest Roman Catholic translations to forsake the Western text-type in favor of the Alexandrian (#2). Of course, it lies outside the Tyndale tradition, though it does have a faint connection with the Douai tradition of Roman Catholic translations (#1).

Jerusalem Bible

The JB is also of Roman Catholic doctrinal orientation, raising the same doctrinal red-flag for non-Roman Catholics as does the NAB (#4). Its philosophy of translation is much freer than that of the New American Bible, however (#3). It falls in the range of free translations rather than that of literal ones. Its English flows smoothly, though it may favor the type of English spoken on the European side of the Atlantic Ocean (#5). Its textual basis is good, but having been translated first from a French translation before being compared to the Hebrew, Aramaic, and Greek of the original, it faces questions about what influence the French text had on the English renderings (#2). It is quite separate from the tradition of Tyndale as well as from any other tradition (#1).

New Jerusalem Bible

The NJB, like its predecessor the JB, is Roman Catholic doctrinally in viewing Peter as the rock on whom the church is built, though at times it appears to favor a theologically liberal outlook about such things as the virgin birth (#4). Neither does it support the perpetual virginity of Mary when it refers to Jesus' brothers and sisters in the Gospels. Its attempt to use gender-neutral language represents a doctrinal weakness in the area of Bibliology. In replacing the JB, one of the freest of the free translations, with a translation that is closer to the original, it represents a vast improvement in translation philosophy (#3). It is almost literal enough to earn a place among the formal-equivalence translations. The highly interpretive nature of the JB was one factor that prompted the NJB revision to be undertaken. Interpretation is still excessive in the NJB, but it is less misleading in this regard than the JB. The translators of the NJB were far less dependent on the French than were those of the JB, causing the NJB to rest on a sounder textual basis (#2). The English style of the NJB flows well, though some readers will find the name 'Yahweh' used to translate the Old Testament Tetragrammaton a little strange (#5). Practically all other translations except the JB use 'LORD' for that purpose. The only historical lineage that the NJB can claim is the JB and the French translation *La Bible de Jerusalem*, on which both English translations are based (#1).

Today's English Version

The TEV, often called the Good News Bible, was the original showpiece of the United Bible Societies for the dynamic-equivalence approach to translating (#3). Since it was one of the earliest such translations sponsored by a large organization, many favored it as a translation for a while. Its location well within the range of free translations sharply reduces its usefulness as a text for serious study. Its textual basis is Alexandrian, which speaks in its favor (#2), but its theological orientation is questionable for the evangelical in areas of Bibliology and Christology (e.g., Phil. 2:6) (#4). It is high-quality contemporary English, but an English that dated itself (#5). The advent of its successor, the Contemporary English Version, has reflected that. The TEV is a tradition all to itself, not being a revision of an earlier translation (#1).

Contemporary English Version

The CEV is a descendant of the TEV in being produced by the American Bible Society also, but apart from that relationship it lies outside any significant lineage of translations (#1). Its major claim to significance is the extra care given to assuring that the translation can be easily *heard* as compared to being *read* (#5). For theological expressions such as 'righteousness', 'redemption', 'atonement', and 'sanctification' it has substituted more widely understood expressions such as 'how God accepts everyone', 'we could come to God', 'make him completely yours', and the like (#5). Its relatively recent appearance (1995) has not allowed time to measure how well it has met that objective. Of course, the 'easily understood' objective has a negative effect of distancing the translation further from the original languages, so that the CEV is well into the free-translation range (#3). Like most other twentieth-century translations, its textual basis is along the lines of the Alexandrian text-type, a point in its favor (#2). Its objective of incorporating gender-neutral language is one of the indications of its loosened view of Bibliology and the generally loosened theological stance that it takes (#4).

The Modern Language Bible
The MLB is independent of the Tyndale tradition, its only ancestor being the Berkeley Version of the New Testament that preceded the whole Bible by fourteen years (#1). At points the MLB follows a literal approach to translation, but sometimes it becomes a little freer (#3). Overall, it belongs in the literal translation range. It is Alexandrian in textual basis (#2) and theologically conservative in its leanings, though it shows some inclination toward amillennial theology (#4). The English usage is inconsistent because different translators produced different books of the Old Testament (#5).

Phillips Modern English and the Living Bible
Most Bible users consider PME and the LB to have translation philosophies that are too free to be useful for anything except evangelistic outreach, though many consult them from time to time for alternate wording in particular passages (#3). They are both beyond the free-translation range, with the LB showing more freedom than Phillips. The textual basis of the two is the same, Alexandrian (#2). Neither has a historical lineage, each originating with a single individual (#1). The LB is more conservative in its theological outlook than Phillips (#4). Phillips came to a more conservative view of inspiration through his translation efforts, but he never

embraced a verbal, plenary view of inspiration. The English usage of each is attractive to many, although the LB tends to become almost vulgar at times (#5).

The New Living Translation
The NLT resulted when Tyndale House Publishers asked a group of biblical scholars to take the Living Bible out of the paraphrase range and make of it a free translation. That the team of scholars did, their product falling about midway into the range of dynamic-equivalent translations (#3). Except for the LB, the NLT has no historical lineage (#1). As most other recent translations, it commendably rests on an Alexandrian text-type (#2). In general, the NLT is conservative in its theological stance, but it is weak in its Bibliology because of an effort to be gender neutral (#4). Its usage of English is contemporary, favoring the English spoken in the United States (#5).

The Message
In reference to its technique of translation, the MES falls well within the range of paraphrases, more free than PME but not as free as the LB (#3). It has proven to be quite popular, particularly among younger readers. Its usefulness is as a devotional aid, but it is essentially useless as a study Bible. The MES has no historical lineage, but is the result of a Presbyterian pastor's effort to recast the New Testament in street language (#1). Its textual basis has more Byzantine-type readings than other recent translations except the Living Bible, but the Alexandrian class of readings is still dominant as the basis for the MES (#2). It reflects a Roman Catholic theological bias in Matthew 16, but this is probably unintentional on the part of the translator (#4). It is generally in the conservative camp theologically. The reading-level of the MES is at a fifth-grade level (#5).

The New English Translation
Like the majority of other late twentieth-century translations, the NET is without a historical lineage (#1). Its textual basis is heavily weighted toward the Alexandrian family of texts (#2). It falls within the dynamic-equivalent range in its translation philosophy, though in many instances it offers a literal rendering of passages in footnotes (#3). The NET commits the same bibliological error of trying to incorporate gender-neutral language as do a number of recent translations (#4). It also commits in the direction of Progressive Dispensationalism in some of its notes, but its theological bias is generally conservative. The English used flows reasonably well, but is not as polished as in some other free translations (#5).

In the brief highlights sketched above, readers may recognize my preferences in each of the five categories of discussion and may choose to disagree. If historical background is not that important to them, they may rate a version in the opposite way (#1). If they prefer a Byzantine textual basis, their choices will be different (#2). If they want a Bible for purely devotional reading, formal-equivalence translations will rank low instead of high (#3). If they are more theologically liberal in orientation, an evangelical bias will not be that important to them (#4). In the matter of English usage, tastes vary so widely that it is difficult to predict what a person will like (#5).

Rating all versions in every respect has been impossible in a work of limited scope. The objective has been to get 'Mr/Mrs/Miss Average Christian' started, however, in thinking about what to look for and in passing judgments of his/her own. After all, this is one of the most significant decisions a person will make in the Christian life: 'Which Bible shall I choose?'

APPENDIX

APPENDIX

DYNAMIC EQUIVALENCE:
A METHOD OF TRANSLATION
OR A SYSTEM OF HERMENEUTICS?

The recent popularity of Dynamic Equivalence in translating the Bible justifies a closer scrutiny of it, particularly in light of the growing interest in biblical hermeneutics that it parallels. A comparison of the disciplines of D-E translation and hermeneutics reveals a large amount of similarity between the two. The similarity exists whether one compares D-E to traditional hermeneutics or to theories being advanced in contemporary hermeneutics. In view of the close parallel between D-E and hermeneutics, three questions need to be faced: a linguistic one, an ethical one, and a practical one.

* * * * *

Dynamic Equivalence (D-E) entered the scene as a formalized method of translation and as a scientific discipline with a theoretical basis about two decades ago, but its presence as a practical pursuit in translating the Bible into English dates back to around the turn of the century.[1] Since the 1960s, it has grown rapidly in popularity and has been greatly

---

[1]E. A. Nida, *Toward a Science of Translating, with Special Reference to Principles and Procedures Involved in Bible Translating* (Leiden: Brill, 1964) 5. Nida noted that the art of translation had outstripped the theory of translation. His work was put forth as an effort to provide a theoretical basis for what was already being produced. In his survey of the history of translation in the western world he writes, 'The 20th century has witnessed a radical change in translation principles' (21). Later in the same work he adds, 'The present direction is toward increasing emphasis on dynamic

acclaimed.[2] This investigation purposes to examine the extent
to which dynamic equivalence draws upon hermeneutical
principles as a part of its translation method and to weigh
whether it should be termed a method of translation or a
system of hermeneutics. Eugene A. Nida, who probably has
earned the title of 'the father of dynamic equivalence', though
he more recently has chosen to call the process 'functional
equivalence',[3] sees hermeneutics as entirely separate from
dynamic-equivalence translation procedures,[4] but does so on
the basis of a novel understanding of hermeneutics. He
defines the field of hermeneutics as that which points out
parallels between the biblical message and present-day events
and determines the extent of relevance and the appropriate
response for the believer.[5]

That concept of hermeneutics is quite different from that
traditionally assigned to the word. Normally it is defined as

---

equivalence. This represents a shift of emphasis which began during the early decades
of this century' (160). Perhaps he was looking back to the *Twentieth Century New
Testament* (1902) as the first effort which utilized what he chooses to label 'dynamic
equivalence' principles. F. F. Bruce, *History of the English Bible* (3rd ed.; New York:
Oxford, 1978) 153, calls this 1902 publication the first of a series of 'modern English
translations'.

[2]E. H. Glassman, *The Translation Debate—What Makes a Bible Translation
Good?* (Downers Grove: InterVarsity, 1981), devotes his work to showing the virtues
of what he calls 'content-oriented' translations, another name for dynamic-equivalent
translations. J. R. Kohlenberger III, *Words about the Word—A Guide to Choosing
and Using Your Bible* (Grand Rapids: Zondervan, 1987) 61-72, also presents an
apologetic for the dynamic equivalence approach. D. A. Carson, 'The Limits of
Dynamic Equivalence in Bible Translation,' *Notes on Translation* 121 (Oct 1987): 1,
hails the triumph of dynamic equivalence in these words: 'As far as those who
struggle with biblical translation are concerned, dynamic equivalence has won the
day—and rightly so.'

[3]J. de Waard and E. A. Nida, *From One Language to Another, Functional
Equivalence in Bible Translating* (Nashville: Nelson, 1986) vii-viii. The authors
mean nothing different from what Nida intended by 'dynamic equivalence' in his
Toward a Science of Translating, but have opted for the new terminology because of
a misunderstanding of the older expression and because of abuses of the principle of
dynamic equivalence by some translators.

[4]E. A. Nida and W. D. Reyburn, *Meaning Across Culture* (Maryknoll, NY: Orbis,
1981) 30.

[5]*Ibid.*

'the science of interpretation'.[6] *Webster's New Collegiate Dictionary* defines hermeneutics as 'the study of the methodological principles of interpretation'.[7] *Webster's New Twentieth Century Dictionary Unabridged* makes hermeneutics synonymous with exegesis.[8] Terry more precisely notes that hermeneutics constitutes the principles of interpretation that are applied by exegesis.[9] Yet Nida emphatically distinguishes between exegesis and hermeneutics, and says they are two distinct components of the larger category of interpretation.[10]

Admittedly the connotation of 'hermeneutics' has shifted in recent times,[11] creating widespread confusion. Yet Nida appears to be in disharmony with everyone in his definition. He has equated hermeneutics with what has traditionally been called 'application', which is based on the one correct

---

[6]M. S. Terry, *Biblical Hermeneutics* (Grand Rapids: Zondervan, n.d.) 17. H. A. Virkler, *Hermeneutics—Principles and Processes of Biblical Interpretation* (Grand Rapids: Baker, 1981) 16, calls hermeneutics 'the science and art of biblical interpretation'. D. F. Ferguson, *Biblical Hermeneutics, an Introduction* (Atlanta: John Knox, 1986) 4, views the traditional definition of hermeneutics as the 'study of the locus and principles of interpretation'.

[7]*Webster's New Collegiate Dictionary* (Springfield, Mass.: G. & C. Merriam, 1983) 536.

[8]*Webster's New Twentieth Century Dictionary of the English Language Unabridged* (New York: Simon and Schuster, 1979) 851. *Webster's Third New International Dictionary of the English Language Unabridged* (Springfield, Mass.: G. & C. Merriam, 1971) 1059, defines hermeneutics as follows: 'the study of the methodological principles of interpretation and explanation; specif.: the study of the general principles of biblical interpretation.'

[9]Terry, *Biblical Hermeneutics* 19.

[10]Nida and Reyburn, *Meaning* 30. See also de Waard and Nida, *From One Language* 40, where the authors write, 'This issue of the communicative role of the Bible highlights an important distinction which may be made between exegesis and hermeneutics, although some writers use these terms almost indistinguishably.'

[11]B. L. Ramm and others, *Hermeneutics* (Grand Rapids: Baker, 1987) 6. Ramm writes, 'Although traditionally hermeneutics has been treated as a special theological discipline, recent studies have endeavored to enlarge the scope of hermeneutics. These studies wish to see hermeneutics in a wider perspective as a function of the human understanding . . .' (6). Ferguson notes that the traditional definition 'needs amplification and qualification since there has been a steady shifting of emphases in carrying out the hermeneutical task . . .' (*Biblical Hermeneutics* 4).

interpretation of the original writing,[12] and in so doing, has represented an extreme position that is unacceptable because it represents an abnormal sense of the word. So his strict dissociation of hermeneutics and translation cannot be taken seriously.

In light of current confusion over the scope of hermeneutics we must stipulate our meaning of the term in the context of this investigation. In the earlier part of the discussion we will focus on 'the more technical kind of hermeneutics known as sacred or biblical hermeneutics',[13] in other words, the traditional definition. Later we will expand to include more recent elements which have in some circles found their way under the broadened umbrella of 'hermeneutics'.

DYNAMIC EQUIVALENCE AND TRADITIONAL HERMENEUTICS

The Overlapping of Dynamic Equivalence and Exegesis
One of the striking features of dynamic equivalence is its embracing within its methodology of what has been known traditionally as biblical exegesis. Inclusion of exegetical procedures is necessitated by the first of three steps that dynamic-equivalence theory recommends. The three steps are reduction of the source text to its structurally simplest and most semantically evident kernels, transference of the meaning from the source language to the receptor language on a structurally simple level, and generation of the stylistically and semantically equivalent expression in the receptor language.[14]

The first of the three steps consists of two parts, analysis of the source text in terms of grammatical relationships and

---

[12]Terry, *Biblical Hermeneutics* 600.

[13]Ramm, *Hermeneutics* 6.

[14]Nida, *Toward a Science* 68. According to Nida, this three-step process is the way 'the really competent translator' works.

analysis of it in terms of the meanings of the words and combinations of words.[15] A common way to illustrate grammatical analysis is with uses of the Greek genitive case and the corresponding English construction of two nouns or pronouns connected by 'of.'[16] Those familiar with the earliest stages of New Testament Greek study recognize quickly that an analysis of the various uses of the Greek genitive case is a standard part of preparation for biblical exegesis. Yet there is a strange reticence by those who espouse D-E methodology to recognize that this type of study has been underway for a long time.[17]

The 1986 work by de Waard and Nida does refer to standard tools of lexicography, but it casts them in a negative light. They label traditional bilingual dictionaries as deficient because such dictionaries depend almost entirely on

---

[15]E. A. Nida and C. R. Taber, *The Theory and Practice of Translation* (Leiden: E. J. Brill, 1969) 33.

[16]Nida, *Toward a Science* 207-8, 229; Nida and Taber, *The Theory* 35-37. 'Field of blood' (Acts 1:19) and 'God of peace' (Phil 4:9) are two among the suggested examples of ambiguity (Nida, 229). For the former Nida suggests two possible interpretations, 'field where blood was spilled' (or 'shed') or 'field that reminded people of blood'. For the latter he rejects 'a peaceful God' as an option, and chooses 'God who gives peace' or 'God who causes peace'.

[17]The sole use of 'exegesis' in the index of Nida's *Toward a Science of Translating* is in a passing reference to the field in his historical survey of translations in the western world (Nida, *Toward a Science* 28). The only place where Nida and Taber use 'exegesis' in their *Theory and Practice of Translation*, according to their index, is as a part of a sample set of principles prepared for use in making a 'Southern Bantu' translation, and this mention is only in passing (Nida and Taber, *The Theory* 182). The standard grammars for New Testament Greek are never alluded to in the above works, nor are they listed in their bibliographies.

This coolness toward what has been a long established field of biblical studies is perhaps reflected in the judgment of Nida and others that good exegetes and grammarians make poor translators (E. A. Nida, 'Bible Translation for the Eighties,' *International Review of Mission* 70 [1981]: 136-137). H. H. Hess, 'Some Assumptions,' a paper read at the President's Luncheon, Biola University, Nov 15, 1984, 9, states as his ninth assumption 'that the linguistic and cultural demands of non-Indo-European languages necessitate biblical interpretation that goes beyond traditional and conventional exegesis'. This assumption of a Wycliffe Bible translator displays the same dissatisfaction with traditional exegesis that Nida and his associates seem to entertain.

'glosses', i.e., surface structure transfer of meanings.[18] The same authors criticize Bauer-Arndt-Gingrich-Danker for being very unsystematic and in failing to cover the ranges of meaning of individual words.[19] It is evident from these criticisms that the analysis step in the D-E process covers the same ground that traditionally has been covered by exegesis, an exegesis based on principles of interpretation that compose the field of hermeneutics.[20]

From the perspective of a traditional definition of hermeneutics little doubt can be entertained that D-E is, among other things, a system of hermeneutics. Perhaps some will respond, however, that all translations are commentaries and hence incorporate the application of hermeneutical principles in arriving at their renderings. This is absolutely true.[21] A certain degree of interpretation is unavoidable, no matter how hard the translator tries to exclude it. Yet a characteristic of formal equivalence is its effort to avoid interpretation as much as possible by transferring directly from the surface structure of the source language to the surface structure of the receptor language.[22] By omitting the

---

[18]de Waard and Nida, *From One Language* 160.

[19]*Ibid.*, 161-62.

[20]Further evidence of the inclusion of hermeneutics in the D-E methodology is seen in what D-E authors have written about such things as how to handle the synonyms ἀγαπάω (*agapaō*, 'I love') and φιλέω (*phileō*, 'I love') in John 21:15-19 (de Waard and Nida, *From One Language* 93), the treatment of anacolutha (*ibid.*, 105), the meaning of καταλαμβάνω (*katalambanō*, 'I apprehend') in John 1:5 (*ibid.*, 107), and the meaning of μαρτυρία Ἰησοῦ (*marturia Iēsou*, 'the testimony of Jesus') in Revelation 1:2 (*ibid.*, 127). All these belong properly in the realm of exegesis. As a matter of fact, de Waard and Nida in essence acknowledge the essential presence of the science of interpretation in D-E when they write, 'The primary exegetical perspective of a translator is "what did the text mean to the people who were the original receptors?" ' (*ibid.*, 177).

Glassman gives a similar but simpler explanation of the step of analysis, using σάρξ (*sarx*, 'flesh') with its varying New Testaments meanings as one of his examples of the interpretive decisions which must be made by a D-E translator (Glassman, *Translation Debate* 59-60).

[21]D. G. Rossetti expressed this over a century ago: 'A translation remains perhaps the most direct form of commentary' (cited by Nida, *Toward a Science* 156).

step of analysis that is built into the D-E approach, interpretation can be excluded to a much higher degree. Since D-E intentionally incorporates interpretation, it obviously has a significantly higher degree of interpretation than formal equivalence and is in a much stronger sense a system of hermeneutics than is formal equivalence.

Dynamic Equivalence and Ambiguous Passages
One type of passage illustrates particularly well the commitment of dynamic equivalence to the practice of hermeneutics. This is a passage whose interpretation is uncertain, i.e., one whose meaning is ambiguous. As a general rule, dynamic equivalence dedicates itself to the elimination of ambiguities.

In building his rationale for D-E, Nida quotes Alexander Fraser Tytler's principle approvingly: 'To imitate the obscurity or ambiguity of the original is a fault and it is still a greater one to give more than one meaning.'[23] To follow through with this perspective, he later uses the Greek genitive-case form with the corresponding use of the English preposition 'of' to illustrate how to eliminate ambiguities.[24] 'Cup of the Lord' (1 Cor 10:21) is rendered 'the cup by which we remember the Lord', 'wisdom of words' (1 Cor 1:17) is taken to be 'well arranged words', and 'sons of wrath' (Eph 2:3) becomes 'those with whom God is angry'.[25] In each case the obscurity in meaning disappears through a grammatical restructuring.[26]

---

[22]W. L. Wonderly, *Bible Translations for Popular Use* (London: United Bible Societies, 1968) 51, calls formal correspondence, a later name for formal equivalence, 'the direct transfer technique'. He refers to dynamic equivalence as a process of 'indirect transfer, involving "decomposition and recomposition" or analysis-plus-restructuring' (*ibid.*).

[23]A. F. Tytler, *The Principles of Translation* (1790), cited by Nida, *Toward a Science* 19.

[24]Nida, *Toward a Science* 207-208; cf. also Nida and Taber, *The Theory* 35-37; Wonderly, *Bible Translations* 163.

[25]*Ibid.*

[26]Wonderly in 1968 noted the rarity of an expression that is ambiguous when its

More recently, de Waard and Nida have expressed the same perspective regarding ambiguous passages: 'It is unfair to the original writer and to the receptors to reproduce as ambiguities all those passages which may be interpreted in more than one way.'[27] They add that the translator should place in the text the best attested interpretation and provide in marginal notes the appropriate alternatives.[28]

Usually the case for non-ambiguity is buttressed by references to the inadequacies of formal-equivalence translations. D-E proponents have multiplied examples of ambiguous and allegedly misleading formal-equivalence translations. The volume of examples adduced have won the case for D-E in the minds of some.[29] As persuasive as these lists are, however, superficiality and carelessness have marked the choices of at least some of the illustrations. The scope of the present discussion permits citation of only one widely used passage to illustrate this. In Psalm 1:1 Glassman cites the description of the 'blessed man' who in formal-equivalence translations does 'not stand in the way of sinners'. He then criticizes the rendering in these words:

---

total context is taken into account (Wonderly, *Bible Translations* 162). He conversely observed that a completely 'unambiguous' expression is also rare (*ibid.*). In light of this he saw the elimination of all potential ambiguities as undesirable. Yet, for the sake of the uneducated, he advised the translator 'to eliminate them or reduce to a minimum the probability of their being misunderstood' (*ibid.*, 163).

Determination to eliminate ambiguities has seemingly grown stronger with the passage of time. In 1981 Nida and Reyburn saw attempts to reproduce ambiguities in a translation as unjust to the original author and unfair to the untrained reader (Nida and Reyburn, *Meaning* 7-8; ambiguities referred to are, of course, those resulting from the scholars' lack of understanding, not intentional ambiguities intended by an author; see also Jean-Claude Margot, 'Should a Translation of the Bible Be Ambiguous,' *BT* 32/4 [Oct 1981]: 406-413). They suggested that the translator's goal should be to translate so as to prevent misunderstanding of what the original receptors understood (*ibid.*, 29).

Also in 1981 Glassman gave 'avoid ambiguity' as one of five guidelines to be followed in correct translation. He displays much less caution in his application of this principle than Wonderly did earlier (Glassman, *The Translation Debate* 101-4).

[27]de Waard and Nida, *From One Language* 39.

[28]*Ibid.*

[29]E.g. Carson, 'The Limits' 1.

'Nowadays to stand in the way of something or someone means to prevent or hinder, to serve as an obstacle.'[30] He should have indicated that this was only a personal opinion because his statement is blatantly inaccurate according to authorities on the English language. Webster's unabridged dictionary gives the following as the first definition of the expression 'in the way of ': 'so as to meet or fall in with; in a favorable position for doing or getting.'[31] This is clearly the correct idea conveyed by the Hebrew, that of 'associate with'. The blessed man does not place himself in a compromising position with sinners.

Unfortunately the reaction of Glassman and others against a formal-equivalence rendering of Psalm 1:1 is characteristic of other ill-advised conclusions by D-E advocates. This is surprising, for some of these are leading linguists who as a part of their methodology advocate a careful respect for the referential meanings of words and expressions as they appear in dictionary resources.[32] Yet they disregard their own advice. For example, de Waard and Nida object to formal-equivalence renderings of Psalm 23:1, 'The Lord is my shepherd, I shall not want,' by stating flatly, 'want no longer means "to lack" but rather "to desire".'[33] In contrast, contemporary dictionaries give the intransitive verb 'want' a

---

[30]Glassman, *Translation Debate* 108. Carson, 'The Limits' 5, and de Waard and Nida, *From One Language* 33, use the same illustration. Glassman is cited because his work has the earliest publication date, though he had access to the unpublished manuscript of de Waard and Nida (Glassman, *Translation Debate* 127 [ch 6, n 7]) and may have obtained it from them.

[31]*Webster's New Twentieth Century* 2071. This same source gives as the first definition of 'in the way' the idea of obstructing, impeding, or hindering, but 'in the way of' is a separate entry (*ibid.*). *Webster's New Collegiate Dictionary*, on the other hand, defines 'in the way' as meaning, first of all, 'in a position to be encountered by one: in or along one's course' (1325). The idea of hindrance or obstruction is not introduced until the second definition in this latter source. Similarly, *Webster's Third New International Dictionary* defines 'in the way' as follows: 'on or along one's path, road, or course: in a position to be encountered by one' (2588).

[32]Nida, *Toward a Science* 70.

[33]de Waard and Nida, *From One Language* 9.

first meaning of 'lack' or 'have a need',[34] exactly what the psalmist intended to say.[35] Rather than correcting the formal-equivalence translators, the linguistic specialists should have acknowledged the legitimacy of their word choice. They would also have been more credible if they had prefaced their critical remark with 'in our sphere of knowledge' or 'according to our judgment', but to say without qualification 'want no longer means "to lack" ' raises questions about their judgment in general.

Formal-equivalence translations handle ambiguities in exactly the opposite way. In the receptor rendering they maintain as far as possible the same ambiguity that exists in the source language. This places a heavier responsibility upon the reader and student of the English text by forcing him either to interpret the passage himself or to resort to a commentary or Bible teacher or expositor for help, but it also leaves open interpretive options that would otherwise be beyond his reach.[36] It also runs less risk of excluding a correct interpretation.

DYNAMIC EQUIVALENCE
AND CONTEMPORARY HERMENEUTICS

To compare dynamic equivalence with contemporary hermeneutics, it is necessary to sketch some of the recent trends in the latter field.

---

[34]*Webster's New Twentieth Century* 2059. *Webster's New Collegiate* gives 'to be needy or destitute' as the first meaning and 'to have or feel need' as the second (1327). The definition incorporating the idea of 'desire' is not given until the fourth definition. After giving an obsolete definition, *Webster's Third New International Dictionary* defines 'want' by 'to be in need' in the first non-obsolete meaning.

[35]Another formal equivalence rendering such as 'lack' may be clearer in the minds of some than 'want', but 'want' is still a very legitimate option.

[36]J. W. Scott, 'Dynamic Equivalence and Some Theological Problems in the NIV,' *WTJ* 48 (Fall 1986): 355, points out the superiority of the KJV and NASB renderings of Acts 16:31 to that in the NIV, in this regard. Translators with limited understanding of the text, he notes, will more probably convey the original meaning

Recent Trends in Hermeneutics
One of the recent foci in hermeneutical discussions is the establishment of a starting point for interpretation. Special attention to this aspect of interpretation furnishes a convenient approach to comparing D-E with contemporary hermeneutics.

This starting point, sometimes called the interpretive center, functions as a control for the interpreter as he attempts to bring together diverse texts of Scripture.[37] It serves as the organizing principle, furnishing the interpretive structure for exegesis, and is therefore a very important consideration.

Eitel portrays two broad types of hermeneutical controls, a Scripture-dominant one and a context-dominant one.[38] These two are a convenient way to divide the wide assortment of starting points that have been proposed. One group belongs to the past and focuses on elements in the original settings of various portions of Scripture, and the other belongs to the present with elements of the contemporary world setting the tone for interpretation.

Thiselton insists that the starting point must be something in the present situation of the interpreter.[39] The interpreter addresses his initial questions to the text and is personally

---

more accurately and more completely than those of a free or D-E translation (see also p. 351). E. L. Miller, 'The New International Version on the Prologue of the John,' *HTR* 72/3-4 (July-Oct 1979): 309, criticizes the NIV for not retaining the ambiguity of the Greek in its handling of John 1:9, saying that the translators had usurped the reader's right to an accurate rendering of the text. J. C. Jeske, 'Faculty Review of the Revised NIV,' *Wisconsin Lutheran Quarterly* 85/2 (Spring 1988): 106, cites the same version for its failure to retain the ambiguity of the Greek text in Hebrews 9:14. Yet he also commends the NIV for retaining ambiguity in its handling of Luke 17:20 (105). A. H. Nichols (in 'Explicitness in Translation and the Westernization of Scripture,' *Reformed Theological Review* 3 [Sept-Dec 1988]: 78-88) calls this focus of D-E 'explicitness' and pinpoints the difficulties it creates in translation.

[37]D. M. Scholer, 'Issues in Biblical Interpretation,' *EQ* LX:1 (Jan 1988): 16.

[38]K. E. Eitel, 'Contextualization: Contrasting African Voices,' *Criswell Theological Review* 2:2 (Spring 1988) 324.

[39]A. C. Thiselton, 'The New Hermeneutic,' *New Testament Interpretation* (Grand Rapids: Eerdmans, 1977) 315.

interpreted by the response of the text, thus beginning the hermeneutical circle.[40] Thiselton criticizes the traditional method according to which the interpreter works with the text as a passive object, making it his starting point. This, he says, is impossible.[41]

Among others who have joined Thiselton in making something in the present a controlling factor in hermeneutics are a number of cross-cultural communication leaders. Padilla is even more specific about the necessity of an interpreter's starting from his own situation.[42] Kraft agrees and notes that different cultural backgrounds produce different needs, which in turn prompt the seeker to ask different questions.[43] Because of this, he continues, new theologies will eventually emerge in non-Western cultures. Revelation is thus a relative matter, differing in each culture and necessitating that interpretation begin with needs formulated by the interpreter.[44]

Marxism as an ideological system is the hermeneutical starting point for liberation theology.[45] Another proposed contemporary starting point in hermeneutics is natural revelation. Mbiti sees natural revelation deposited in African religions as equal in authority with and therefore in control of biblical revelation.[46] Bruce Narramore places natural revelation through secular psychology on the same level of authority as biblical revelation and interprets the Bible through the eyes of secular psychological theory.[47] This list of

---

[40]*Ibid.*, 316.

[41]*Ibid.*; A. C. Thiselton, *The Two Horizons* (Grand Rapids: Eerdmans, 1980) 87.

[42]C. R. Padilla, 'The Interpreted Word: Reflections on Contextual Hermeneutics,' *Themelios* 7/1 (1981): 22.

[43]C. H. Kraft, *Christianity in Culture* (Maryknoll, NY: Orbis, 1979) 144-46.

[44]*Ibid.*

[45]Ferguson, *Biblical Hermeneutics* 177.

[46]J. S. Mbiti, 'The Encounter of Christian Faith and African Religion,' *Christian Century* 97 (August 27–September 3, 1980): 817-18.

[47]Bruce Narramore, 'The Isolation of General and Special Revelation as the Fundamental Barrier to the Integration of Faith and Learning,' paper read at

controlling principles could be expanded easily.[48]

The above rapid survey reflects that in the minds of many the traditional starting point in hermeneutics, that of the original text, is no longer acceptable as a control in interpretation, if it ever was. Criticisms of the grammatico-historical method of interpretation are often direct and uninhibited.[49] It is clear that the hermeneutical focus has shifted dramatically from the original setting of Scripture to a variety of contemporary issues that have become interpretative controls.

Trends in Translation

Contemporary trends in translation have paralleled those in hermeneutics. The traditional method of translation adopted the source message as its control and sought to bring the contemporary reader back to that point.[50] Most recent preferences in translation express the opposite goal, that of bringing the source message into the twentieth century to the

---

President's Luncheon, Biola University, Oct 22, 1984, 2-3, 10.

[48]Some representative writers with a feminist emphasis are explicit about interpretive centers pertaining to their present personal situations. Hull starts with the interpretive guideline that women are fully redeemed and formulates her biblical interpretations in this light (G. G. Hull, 'Response,' *Women, Authority and the Bible* [Downers Grove: InterVarsity, 1986] 24). Fiorenza's organizing principle in interpretation is the oppression of women by men (Elisabeth Schussler Fiorenza, *In Memory of Her* [New York: Crossroad, 1984] 32-33). In light of contemporary social emphases Jewett and Bilezikian identify Galatians 3:28 as a norm according to which other Scriptures must be interpreted (P. K. Jewett, *Man as Male and Female* [Grand Rapids: Eerdmans, 1975] 142; G. Bilezikian, *Beyond Sex Roles* [Grand Rapids: Baker, 1985] 128; see also Jerry H. Gill, 'Mediated Meaning: A Contextualist Approach to Hermeneutical Method,' *Asbury Theological Journal* 43/1 [Spring 1988]: 37-38). The conviction that contemporary experience should be identical to apostolic Christianity is another principle that will control interpretation (R. Stronstad, 'Trends in Pentecostal Hermeneutics,' *Paraclete* 22/3 [Summer 1988]: 2-3). Other controls that have been suggested include a decision about whether one can lose his salvation or not, a conviction about non-participation in war, and ideas about the capability of a believer's never sinning (Scholer, 'Issues' 16-17).

[49]E.g. Kraft, *Christianity in Culture* 131, 136-137; W. S. Lasor, 'The Sensus Plenior and Biblical Interpretation,' *Scripture, Tradition, and Interpretation* (Grand Rapids: Eerdmans, 1978) 266; see also Scholer, 'Issues' 9.

[50]Nida, *Toward a Science* 165.

contemporary reader.[51] The new aim is to relate the text to the receptor and his modes of behavior relevant within the context of his own culture, a controlling factor called 'the principle of equivalent effect'.[52] The traditional method of taking the receptor to the text seeks to help the reader identify himself with a person in the source-language context as fully as possible, teaching him the customs, manner of thought, and means of expression of the earlier time. With D-E, comprehension of the patterns of the source-language culture is unnecessary.[53] The prime concern given to effective communication by D-E at the expense of the source is a vivid confirmation of this shift in focus.[54]

These two starting points are quite distinct from each other.

---

[51]*Ibid.*, 166; Glassman, *Translation Debate* 74; H. M Wolf, 'When "Literal" Is Not Accurate,' *The NIV—The Making of a Contemporary Translation* (Grand Rapids: Zondervan, 1986) 127. Jerome's Latin Vulgate has often been used as an early example of dynamic equivalence or idiomatic translation because Jerome expressed the purpose of translating 'sense for sense' rather than 'word for word' (e.g. see Nida, *Toward a Science* 13; J. Beekman and J. Callow, *Translating the Word of God* [Grand Rapids: Zondervan, 1974] 24). This widely used quotation of Jerome is wrongly used, however, because Jerome adds an important qualification to his statement that is not usually noticed: 'except for Holy Scripture where even the word order is sacred' (*Epistle LVII*, in Jerome: Lettres [ed. Jerome Labourt; Paris, 1953] III:59, cited by Harvey Minkoff, 'Problems of Translations: Concern for the Text Versus Concern for the Reader,' *Biblical Review* 4/4 [Aug 1988] 36). *Mysterium*, the Latin word rendered 'sacred' in this quotation, is rendered 'a mystery' by others (Philip Schaff and Henry Wace, *A Select Library of Nicene and Post-Nicene Fathers* [Grand Rapids: Eerdmans, 1954] 6:133), because *mysterium* and *sacramentum* were used almost interchangeably by the Latin Fathers to refer to holy things (A. Dulles, 'Mystery in Theology,' *New Catholic Encyclopedia* [Washington: The Catholic University of America, 1967] 10:152). Regardless of the English rendering of this word, however, the fact remains that because of its inspiration, Jerome put Scripture into a special category that required more literal translation principles than other literature. His Vulgate was therefore quite literal (Minkoff, 'Problems' 36).

[52]*Ibid.*, 159. Minkoff describes formal equivalence in different terminology. It produces a 'text-oriented' or 'overt' translation because of its persuasion that the meaning lies in the text. D-E on the other hand produces a 'reader-oriented' or 'covert' translation, assuming that meaning inheres in audience reaction to the text (Minkoff, 'Problems' 35).

[53]*Ibid.*

[54]D-E does give attention to the source text in its step called 'analysis', which is described above. This is not the prime concern of D-E, however. In its quest for

Formal-equivalence and D-E approaches represent two opposite poles in a clash that sometimes has been labeled 'literal translation' vs. 'free translation'.[55] To be sure, there are many grades or levels between the polar distinctions,[56] but they are polar distinctions. The differing grades between the two poles are traceable to the varying degrees of consistency with which the translators have adhered to their stated goals and to self-imposed limitations upon the full implementation of D-E principles from passage to passage within the translation.

An example of across-the-board dynamic equivalence is *The Cotton Patch Version* produced by Clarence Jordan. It transforms the source text culturally, historically, and linguistically.[57] In this work Annas and Caiaphas are co-presidents of the Southern Baptist Convention. Jesus is born in Gainesville, Georgia, and lynched rather than being crucified. Most, of course, would not push D-E to that extreme.[58] Yet the work still illustrates the direction of D-E. It shows how the methodology is limited only by the judgment of the translator or translators.[59]

---

greater communicative effectiveness, it intentionally omits some information of the source text with all its details (see Nida, *Toward a Science* 224). Perhaps the secondary importance of the source text and its meaning is reflected also in some of Nida's expressions when he injects some of his precautionary remarks. Commending Phillips' translation for its high rate of decodability, he adds, 'Whether Phillips' translation of this passage is the best way of rendering these difficult verses is not the question at this point' (Nida, *Toward a Science* 175-76). This could imply that accuracy in meaning is not the major concern in translation (see also 207-8 where a similar idea is expressed). Nichols sees the plight of D-E as hopeless because it fails to distinguish between translation and communication ('Explicitness' 82-83).

[55]Nida, *Toward a Science* 22, 171.

[56]*Ibid.*, 24.

[57]Nida and Reyburn, *Meaning* 19; Glassman, *Translation Debate* 74. Two translations that are similar to *The Cotton Patch Version* in their across-the-board D-E are *God is for Real, Man* by Carl F. Burke (1966) and *The Word Made Fresh* by Andrew Edington (1975) (S. Kubo and W. F. Specht, *So Many Versions?* [rev. ed.; Grand Rapids: Zondervan, 1983] 330-33).

[58]Nida, *Toward a Science* 184.

[59]For example, de Waard and Nida, *From One Language* 37-39, suggest five

Such a release from restraints of the original text coincides
with varying degrees of subjectivism that characterize
contemporary hermeneutical systems. These recent schemes
dismiss the traditional system of letting the author be the
determining factor in interpretation. In so doing, of necessity
they force a judgment of the Bible's meaning through the eyes
of something or someone contemporary. Hirsch notes that the
text has to represent someone's meaning; if it is not the
author's, then it must be the modern critic's meaning that is
drawn from the text.[60] Hirsch's terminology distinguishes the
author's meaning from the critic's by calling what the author
intended 'meaning' and by using the term 'significance' to
refer to a relationship between that meaning and a person,
concept, situation, or anything else.[61]

Another way of viewing such hermeneutics is by
contrasting it with the traditional hermeneutical distinction
between interpretation and application.[62] Gill, an advocate of
a contextualist approach to hermeneutics, says it quite plainly.
He supposes that his mentor of thirty years ago, Professor
Traina, will disagree with his contextualist method in which
there is no longer a distinction between interpretation and
application.[63] Application has taken a position as a part of
interpretation, and in the case of Jordan's translation, it has
almost replaced interpretation completely.

situations when functional (i.e. dynamic) equivalence rather than formal equivalence
should be used. Carson, 'The Limits' 5-7, suggests that equivalence of response be
limited to linguistic categories alone.

[60]E. D. Hirsch, Jr., *Validity in Interpretation* (New Haven: Yale University, 1967)
3, 5.

[61]Ibid., 8.

[62]M. Silva, *Has the Church Misread the Bible* (Grand Rapids: Zondervan, 1987)
63-67, suggests that application is essentially equivalent to allegorical interpretation.
This suggestion is interesting, but it loses sight of the fact that allegorical
interpretation as usually understood does not change from place to place and period
to period as practical application does. Rather it attaches itself to the text as a deeper
or hidden meaning that is more or less stable.

[63]Gill, 'Mediated Meaning' 40.

Though Nida and others call *The Cotton Patch Version* a translation, Charles Kraft calls it a 'cultural translation' or 'transculturation',[64] but he also concedes that translation is a limited form of transculturation.[65] He agrees with Nida in advocating use of a 'dynamically equivalent' message to secure a response from the modern recipient that is equivalent to the response of the original recipients of the message. Kraft carries dynamic equivalence beyond transculturation into the realm of theologizing, concluding that the latter is a necessary outgrowth of the former.[66] He incorporates social custom as so much of a controlling factor in dynamic-equivalence theologizing that matters like the biblical teachings against polygamy and in favor of monogamous church leadership are negated.[67] This is reminiscent of the hermeneutical use of natural revelation by Mbiti as an equal authority in the interpretation of the Bible.[68] Here then is another tie-in between contemporary hermeneutics and dynamic equivalence.

Other Similarities Between Contemporary Hermeneutics and Dynamic Equivalence

A similarity in origin. It seems appropriate to point out the similarity in source between recent hermeneutical trends and dynamic-equivalence techniques. To a large degree, both have originated in circles that might be labeled as 'missiological', 'cross-cultural', or 'biblical linguistic'. One only needs to recall some of the prominent names from our earlier discussion of hermeneutics to illustrate this. Padilla,

---

[64]Kraft, *Christianity in Culture* 284-86. Kraft has a narrower definition of translation: '... The translator is not free to provide the degree, extent, and specificity of interpretation required to establish the message solidly in the minds of the hearers. Nor is it within the province of a translator to elaborate on the written message to approximate that of spoken communication' (280).

[65]*Ibid.*, 281.

[66]*Ibid.*, 291.

[67]C. H. Kraft, 'Dynamic Equivalence Churches,' *Missiology* 1 (1973): 53-54.

[68]See above p. 174.

Kraft, Mbiti, and others in the listed fields have been in the forefront of the contextualization movement that proposes, among other things, a revamping of traditional hermeneutical principles.[69] As for dynamic equivalence in translation, Nida notes five influences that have changed translation principles in this century.[70] Two of them relate directly to mission organizations, and the other three are indirectly related to mission activities. Grossman concurs regarding the mission-oriented origin, giving major credit to biblical linguists in missions for the insistence that translation be carried out in cultural context as dynamic equivalence advocates.[71]

A similarity of subjectivity. We have mentioned previously the context-dominant approach of contemporary hermeneutics, and have noted the high degree of subjectivism promoted thereby.[72] A similar subjectivity prevails in dynamic equivalence. The potential for interpretational bias is maximized in the D-E approach.[73] Fortunately it has not been used

---

[69]To the above list other names involved in cross-cultural fields could be mentioned: L. W. Caldwell (see 'Third Horizon Ethnohermeneutics: Re-Evaluating New Testament Hermeneutical Models for Intercultural Bible Interpreters Today' [paper presented to Consultation of Anthropologists and Theologians, Biola University, April 14-15, 1986] 2), K. Haleblian (see 'The Problem of Contextualization,' *Missiology: An International Review* 9/1 [Jan 1983]: 99), W. A. Smalley (see 'Culture and Superculture,' *Practical Anthropology* 2 [1955]: 58-69), S. G. Lingenfelter (see 'Formal Logic or Practical Logic: Which Should Form the Basis for Cross-Cultural Theology?' [paper presented at the Consultation of Anthropologists and Theologians, Biola University, Apr 14-15, 1986]: 2, 21), J. M. Bonino (see *Doing Theology in a Revolutionary Situation* [Philadelphia: Fortress, 1975] 88-89), and H. M. Conn (see 'Contextualization: A New Dimension for Cross-Cultural Hermeneutic,' *Evangelical Missions Quarterly* 14 [1978]: 44-45).

[70]Nida, *Toward a Science* 21-22. The five influences are the rapidly expanding field of structural linguistics, the Summer Institute of Linguistics (i.e. Wycliffe Bible Translators), the program of the United Bible Societies, the publication *Babel* by the International Federation of Translators, and machine translators. The second and third are mission organizations, and the other three have impacted the methodology of these and other mission organizations.

[71]Glassman, *Translation Debate* 73-74, 75-76.

[72]See above pp. 173-74, 178.

[73]Nida, *Toward a Science* 184.

often or widely for propaganda purposes, but D-E translations inevitably encounter criticism in various passages because the interpretations chosen in debated passages will always displease some. This problem is not nearly so characteristic of formal-equivalence translations.

The *New International Version* furnishes a good vehicle for illustrating the problem created by subjectivity because, though it is a dynamic-equivalence translation, strict limitations in its application of D-E principles have greatly reduced its deviations from traditional norms of translation.[74] In other words, it differs radically from the extreme dynamic equivalence of *The Cotton Patch Version*, for example. Nevertheless, there is and has been a steady stream of criticism of NIV renderings. A few illustrations will suffice to show this:

(1) In 1976 Mare raised questions about the NIV rendering of σάρξ (*sarx*, 'flesh') in 1 Corinthians 5:5 by 'the sinful nature', saying that in this verse it referred to the body.[75]

(2) In 1979 Miller criticized the NIV when it rendered

---

[74]Because of the nature of the limitations observed in producing the NIV, Scott refers to its methodology as 'moderate "dynamic equivalence" ' (Scott, *Dynamic Equivalence* 351). J. P. Lewis, 'The New International Version,' *ResQ* 24/1 (1981): 6, a member of the NIV translation team, describes the NIV as a compromise between the traditional and the innovative, as sometimes literal and sometimes dynamically equivalent. Yet the purpose of the NIV as stated in its preface, that of representing the meaning rather than producing a word-for-word translation, places this version squarely in the category of D-E ('Preface,' *The New International Version Study Bible* [Grand Rapids: Zondervan, 1985] xi). Kohlenberger calls the NIV a D-E translation (Kohlenberger, *Words* 92). The accuracy of his categorization is confirmed by the extremely complex system of symbols and typefaces used in the exhaustive concordance that attempts to cross-reference the English of that translation with words of the original languages (cf. Edward W. Goodrick and John R. Kohlenberger III, eds., *The NIV Exhaustive Concordance* [Grand Rapids: Zondervan, 1990] ix-xxii).

[75]W. H. Mare, '1 Corinthians,' *EBC* (Grand Rapids: Zondervan, 1976) 217. In a 1984 revision the rendering in the text remains the same, but the NIV committee has added two alternatives: 'his body' and 'the flesh'. Mare's suggested correction is one of many found in the *Expositor's Bible Commentary* which uses the NIV as its basic text.

ἐσκήνωσεν (*eskēnōsen*, 'he dwelled') in John 1:14 by 'lived for a while'. This, he said, goes too far in molding the reader's interpretation.[76]

(3) In the same year Scaer objected to 1 Peter 2:8b in the NIV as an illustration of how this version is potentially more insidious than the Living Bible because doctrinal problems are less easily recognized.[77] The rendering, he said, supported Calvin's doctrine of election to damnation.

(4) In 1980 Fee objected to the NIV's rendering of γυναικὸς ἅπτεσθαι (*gunaikos haptesthai*, '[good] for a woman not to touch') by 'marry' in 1 Corinthians 7:1.[78]

(5) In 1986 Scott criticized the NIV's handling of a number of passages in Acts (i.e., 2:39; 16:34; 18:8) that in the Greek allow for paedobaptism, a possibility that is excluded by NIV renderings in these places.[79]

(6) In 1988, Jeske on behalf of the faculty of Wisconsin Lutheran Seminary voiced dissatisfaction with the NIV's rendering of Matthew 5:32 in both its original form (i.e., 'anyone who divorces his wife, except for marital unfaithfulness, causes her to commit adultery, and anyone who marries a woman so divorced commits adultery') and in its most recently revised form (i.e., 'anyone who divorces his wife, except for marital unfaithfulness, causes her to become

---

[76]Miller, 'The New International Version' 309. The committee responded by changing the rendering to 'made his dwelling' in the 1984 revision.

[77]David P. Scaer, 'The New International Version—Nothing New,' *CTQ* 43/1 (June 1979): 242. The committee has not yet changed this rendering. Nor have they chosen to change the words 'came to life' in Revelation 20:4. Scaer objected to these words because of their millennialistic implications.

[78]G. D. Fee, 'I Corinthians 7:1 in the NIV,' *JETS* 23/4 (1980), 307-314. The committee has not yet incorporated his suggested literal rendering of 'touch a woman', but has left the text as it was with an added alternative in the margin which reads 'have sexual relations with a woman'. In 1990 Fee has gone further and expressed hesitation about D-E in general and the NIV in particular because he found 'far too many absolutely wrong exegetical choices . . . locked into the biblical text as the reader's only option' ('Reflections on Commentary Writing,' *TToday* 46/4 [Jan 1990]: 388).

[79]Scott, 'Dynamic Equivalence' 353-358.

an adulteress, and anyone who marries the divorced woman commits adultery').[80]

Reviewers and exegetes find fault with the NIV as being too interpretive here and there, because interpretation is an inescapable aspect of D-E. Since interpretations differ from person to person, no rendering that limits the possibilities to a single interpretation will please everyone. Some ask, 'Why could not the text have been left ambiguous in this case?'[81] Others suggest dispensing with the D-E approach so that ambiguities in the source text are left ambiguous in the translation throughout.[82] After examining how the NIV handles a number of debated passages, some writers suggest that the NIV may have a somewhat 'free-wheeling' strain throughout.[83]

This dissatisfaction stems ultimately from the large subjective element that is inherent in D-E. Here then is another area of kinship with contemporary hermeneutics. Continuing revision committees are at work on the NIV and similar versions to try to weed out unsatisfactory renderings. The general 'tightening' trend observable in the recommendations of these committees[84] is an implicit recognition of the problems raised by subjectivity. The task is

---

[80]Jeske, 'Faculty Review' 106-7. This list of NIV criticisms may be lengthened by consulting Robert P. Martin, *Accuracy of Translation and the New International Version* (Edinburgh: Banner of Truth, 1989) 41-62.

[81]Jeske, 'Faculty Review' 106-7.

[82]Scaer, 'The New International Version' 243.

[83]Miller, 'The New International Version' 310; Scott, 'Dynamic Equivalence' 361. Kohlenberger, *Words* 66-67, recognizes the problem of the excessive-commentary element in versions such as the *Amplified Bible*, the *Living Bible*, and *Wuest's Expanded Translation*, but he is apparently oblivious to the presence of the same in the NIV. Thomas A. Boogaart criticizes the NIV's sacrificing of faithfulness to the original Hebrew and Greek in the interest of harmonizing different textual traditions within Scripture and of seeking agreement with various scientific theories ('The New International Version: What Price Harmony?' *Reformed Review* 43/3 [Spring 1990]: 189-203).

[84]E.g. Jeske, 'Faculty Review' 104; see also Kubo and Specht, *So Many* 82-83, 253-254.

endless because of the translation philosophy of D-E versions.

A similarity in theological implications. Another relationship between contemporary hermeneutics and D-E in translation is detectable in the theological implications of each. Some have shied away from this subject for fear of saying too much or of being misunderstood. Yet something of this nature must be discussed.

Nida observes the tendency of those who hold the traditional orthodox view of inspiration to focus attention on the autographs and therefore to favor a formal-equivalence approach to translation.[85] On the other hand, he sees those who hold to neo-orthodoxy or who have been influenced by neo-orthodoxy to be freer in their translations. This, he says, is traceable to neo-orthodoxy's view of inspiration in terms of the response of the receptor with a consequent de-emphasis on the source message.[86] He and Reyburn make clear that there are exceptions to this rule, however.[87]

There is little doubt that the assured conviction that the Hebrew, Aramaic, and Greek autographs of the Bible are inspired, lies behind the dominance of formal-equivalence translations throughout the earlier centuries of Christianity. The Philoxenian, Harclean, and Palestinian Syriac Versions are early examples of efforts to conform the translation to the original text for this reason.[88] The theological motive behind this type of translation is obvious.[89]

---

[85]Nida, *Toward a Science* 27.

[86]*Ibid.*

[87]Nida and Reyburn, *Meaning* 61. Kohlenberger is one of those exceptions when he writes, 'I believe in verbal inspiration, but I do not believe a word-for-word translation best honors that view of Scripture' (Kohlenberger, *Words* 73).

[88]B. M. Metzger, *The Early Versions of the New Testament* (New York: Oxford, 1977) 65, 69, 80.

[89]de Waard and Nida, *From One Language* 10. Carson's statement is surprising: 'Why a literal translation is necessarily more in keeping with the doctrine of verbal

The presence of such a motive can be seen in the reactionary nature of some of the early-twentieth-century free translations. Moffatt in the preface of his free translation of the New Testament associates his freedom in translation methodology with being 'freed from the influence of the theory of verbal inspiration'.[90] Phillips justifies his approach in a similar way in the preface to one of his paraphrases: 'Most people, however great their reverence for the New Testament may be, do not hold a word-by-word theory of inspiration ....'[91]

Another symptom of a relaxed attitude toward biblical inspiration is the attitude of D-E advocates toward the source languages of Scripture. Nida and Taber view these languages as being no different from any other languages. They make a strong point that Hebrew and Greek are subject to the same

---

inspiration, I am quite at a loss to know' (D. A Carson, *The King James Version Debate* [Grand Rapids: Baker, 1979] 90). The church has long felt that inspiration elevates the original texts to the point that a translation should reflect as much of them as possible, as reflected in Minkoff's careful analysis of the goals of the LXX translators and Jerome in biblical translation (Minkoff, 'Problems' 35-36).

[90]J. Moffatt, *The New Testament, A New Translation* (1913) vii.

[91]J. B. Phillips, *The Gospels Translated into Modern English* (1952) 5. It may be coincidental, but the earliest formulation of D-E theory coincided with the espousal of new theoretical proposals regarding inspiration among evangelicals. It was just one year before the appearance of Nida's *Toward a Science of Translating* that Earle wrote the following in the ETS Bulletin: 'The words are not the ultimate reality, but the thoughts which they seek to convey . . .' (R. Earle, *Bulletin of the Evangelical Theological Society* 6/1 [Winter 1963]: 16). He continues by observing that Paul's struggle to find adequate words 'accords well with the view of plenary dynamic inspiration—much better than it does with plenary verbal inspiration' (*ibid.*).

It was also roughly contemporary with similar developments in other realms. Just seven years after Nida's initial effort at establishing a theoretical basis for D-E, Richard Buffum, in one of his regular columns of the *Los Angeles Times*, wrote, 'Contemporary journalism is learning to perceive a subtle spectrum of grays between the old black and white reporting techniques' (R. Buffum, *Los Angeles Times* [Oct 5, 1971]). He defines 'subtle spectrum of grays' as a new 'kind of ponderous, informed subjectivity' that journalists are using in place of 'the old rigidly "objective" approach" ' (*ibid.*).

These other developments probably had nothing directly to do with the development of D-E, but they portray the spirit of the age that indirectly spawned the D-E philosophy.

limitations as any other natural language.[92] This point is valid, but it is only part of the picture. These biblical languages are the only ones that God chose to communicate inspired Scripture and are therefore unique among all languages. Why, then, do D-E advocates criticize those who believe in biblical inspiration and put these languages into a special category because of it,[93] unless they themselves hold a lower view of biblical inspiration? How, then, can these same authorities, in a context of discussing Bible translation, insist that anything said in one language can be said in another,[94] when there is inevitably some loss of meaning in translating from the inspired original into other languages? Is there an evangelical rationale for such emphases?

Though opposition by D-E to an evangelical view of inspiration may not be viewed as explicit, there are implications and overtones that raise serious questions. Certainly no doubt can be entertained about the clear evangelical stance of some individuals that have participated in D-E efforts. The question here relates to the foundational philosophy behind D-E.

The same type of questions exists in regard to the hermeneutical emphases of contextualization. For example, the position of Charles Kraft regarding the relative nature of all systematic theology[95] calls into question the traditional doctrine of inspiration with its associated grammatico-historical method of interpretation.[96] Herein lies another

---

[92]Nida and Taber, *The Theory* 7.

[93]Ibid., 3, 6. In discussing D-E, Kraft rejects 'mere literalness even out of reverence for *supposedly sacred words*' (Kraft, 'Dynamic Equivalence' 44 [italics added]). Is this an implicit denial that the words of the original text were inspired?

[94]*Ibid.*, 4.

[95]Kraft, *Christianity in Culture* 291-292.

[96]Article XVIII, 'Articles of Affirmation and Denials, The Chicago Statement on Biblical Inerrancy,' International Council on Biblical Inerrancy (Chicago, 1978); Article XV, 'Articles of Affirmation and Denials, The Chicago Statement on Biblical Hermeneutics,' International Council on Biblical Inerrancy (Chicago, 1982).

similarity of D-E to contemporary hermeneutics.

The two fields can be tied together even more specifically when, now and then, some of the hermeneutical presuppositions of D-E come to light. For example, Nida and Reyburn appear to be in agreement with Smalley regarding the non-absolute nature of biblical revelation. Smalley elaborates on alleged biblical diversity in such a way as to raise questions about his view of inspiration. He notes that Jesus in the antitheses of Matthew 5 revoked the teachings of Moses in the Old Testament and substituted a new standard that was better suited to the Palestinian culture of the first century.[97] Nida and Reyburn accept this proposition that differing cultures have caused contradictory presuppositions in the Bible, citing the same passage as Smalley to prove their assertion.[98] Other contradictions that they cite include the teaching of henotheism in certain parts of the Old Testament and the teaching of monotheism in others, the Old Testament teaching of polygamy as set aside in the New Testament, and the New Testament rejection of the Old Testament sacrificial system.[99]

If this is not an explicit disavowal of an evangelical view of inspiration, it is at best a foggy representation.

QUESTIONS THAT REMAIN

An answer to our initial question of whether D-E is a method of translation or a system of hermeneutics must acknowledge a considerable amount of hermeneutics in the dynamic-equivalence process. The correlation between contemporary

[97]W. A. Smalley, 'Culture and Superculture,' *Practical Anthropology* 2 (1955): 60-62; Kraft, *Christianity in Culture* 126. Evangelical attempts to cope with alleged biblical diversity are usually a little more subtle than Smalley's; see Scholer, 'Issues' 14-18, and I. H. Marshall, 'An Evangelical Approach to "Theological Criticism," ' *Themelios* 13/3 (Apr/May 1988): 79-85.

[98]Nida and Reyburn, *Meaning* 26-27.

[99]*Ibid.*

hermeneutics and dynamic equivalence is not as conspicuous as that between traditional hermeneutics and formal equivalence. Nevertheless, even here substantial similarities exist. Even if one cannot agree to the former correlation, as suggested above, it must be granted that D-E incorporates a large measure of contemporary hermeneutics into its fabric. That being the case, several questions arise.

A Linguistic Question

Nida and other linguistic authorities are quite specific in telling translators to abide by the referential meanings of words, meanings they identify with those found in standard dictionaries.[100] In *Webster's Ninth New Collegiate Dictionary* the relevant definition of the word 'translation' is, 'an act, process, or instance of translating: as **a**: a rendering from one language into another; also the product of such a rendering.'[101] There is little doubt that, in the minds of most people who use the English language, the term 'translation' used in a cross-cultural connection suggests the simple idea of changing from one language into another. Yet this is only one-third of the process of dynamic equivalence, the step that is called 'transfer'.[102] The question is then, 'Is it proper linguistic practice to use the word "translation" to describe the product of a D-E exercise?'[103]

More recently, de Waard and Nida use 'associative

---

[100]Nida, *Toward a Science* 70.

[101]*Webster's Ninth New Collegiate Dictionary* (Springfield, Mass.: Merriam-Webster, 1988) 1254.

[102]Glassman, *The Translation Debate* 61-63.

[103]Glassman equates the verb 'translate' with the verb 'interpret' in his attempt to show the basic equality in meaning of 'translate' and 'paraphrase' (Glassman, *The Translation Debate* 61-63). His definition, however, is limited to the use of 'translate' within the same language rather than its use in connection with different languages. He states his definition in such a way that the noun 'translation' is hardly ever qualified in general usage in connection with D-E. From the perspective of referential meaning, he fails in this regard to justify the use of 'translate' in the senses of 'interpret' or 'paraphrase'.

meaning' in lieu of 'referential meaning' to describe lexical definitions.[104] They point out, for example, the hesitancy of most translations to use 'Yahweh', because in the minds of many Christians, it has become associated with a modernistic attitude toward the Bible and God.[105]

Should not the same precision be shown in use of the word 'translation'? The use of 'translation' to include implementation of all the principles of hermeneutics and exegesis reflects an insensitivity to the associative meaning of that word in the minds of most English-speaking people. Perhaps 'commentary' is too strong a word to describe a D-E product, but it seems that something such as 'cultural translation'[106] or 'interpretive translation' would be more in keeping with principles espoused by linguistic authorities.

An Ethical Question

A closely related ethical question may also be raised: Is it honest to give people what purports to be the closest representation of the inspired text in their own language, yet which is something that intentionally maximizes rather than minimizes the personal interpretations of the translator or translators?

Graves has observed that every translation is a lie in the sense that there are no identical equivalents between languages.[107] This problem is alleviated by an understanding in the minds of most that translation is done by means of near equivalents rather than exact equivalents.[108] But if a translator goes one step further and intentionally incorporates his personal interpretations when he could have left many passages with the same ambiguity as the original, has he done

---

[104]de Waard and Nida, *From One Language* 123-24.
[105]*Ibid.*, 142.
[106]Kraft, *Christianity in Culture* 284-286.
[107]R. Graves, 'The Polite Lie,' *The Atlantic* 215 (June 1965): 80.
[108]Glassman, *The Translation Debate* 75.

right by those who will use his translation?

It is not our purpose to pursue this ethical question further, but simply to raise it as a matter for possible discussion.

A Practical Question

A last question for consideration relates to the use of a D-E product in ministry: How shall I deal with the problem that the high degree of interpretation in a D-E work makes it unsuitable for close study by those who do not know the original languages?[109] The answer to this question will depend on the type of preaching and teaching they do. If their approach is general, dealing only with broad subjects, they perhaps will not be too bothered by this characteristic.

But if they at times treat specific doctrinal issues and want to stress this or that detail of the text, the presence of a large interpretive element in the basic text will pose problems. They will inevitably encounter renderings that differ from the view they want to represent in their message—a problem that is largely precluded in using a formal-equivalence translation. If a preacher has to correct his translation too often, people will soon look upon it as unreliable and reflect doubts about either the translation itself or the larger issue of biblical inspiration.

These are only three questions that emerge because of an intentional incorporation of hermeneutics into the translation process. Others could be proposed. It seems that precision in

---

[109]There is agreement among those who have faced the issue, that free translations and paraphrases are inadequate for those who wish to do a detailed study of the English text (J. P. Lewis, *The English Bible/from KJV to NIV* [Grand Rapids: Baker, 1981] 116, 156, 260, 291; Kubo and Specht, *So Many* 80, 150, 242, 338; W. LaSor, 'Which Bible is Best for You?' *Eternity* 25 [Apr. 1974] 29). For a detailed discussion of the 'Practical Question', see Robert L. Thomas, 'Bible Translations: The Link Between Exegesis and Expository Preaching,' *The Master's Seminary Journal* 1/1 (Spring 1990): 53-73.

discussing English versions of the Bible has largely been lost. If more exact terminology is not adopted, the church may some day incur the besetting ailment of a confusion of tongues that is self-inflicted.

Persons Index

Scripture Index

Subject Index